Hearing Form

Hearing Form is a textbook for upper-level undergraduate college courses on the analysis of musical forms. It reviews concepts such as score reading, instrumental transposition, cadences, phrase structure, harmonic sequences, and modulation while at the same time introducing a style of phrase diagramming and an approach to hearing without the score that is used consistently throughout the book. The goal of this book is to teach students to:

- Identify phrase endings and cadence types in music with or without a score.
- Identify harmonic sequence types in music with or without a score.
- Identify modulations in music with or without a score.
- Identify formal sections in music with or without a score.
- Identify musical forms with or without a score.

Hearing Form is a complete course. It is a textbook and workbook with a separate score anthology. The companion website provides musical examples that can be downloaded for selected pieces in the anthology.

Matthew Santa is Associate Professor of Music Theory and Chair of Music Theory and Composition at the Texas Tech University School of Music. He is also currently serving as President of the Texas Society for Music Theory.

www.routledge.com/textbooks/9780415872638

Hearing Form

Musical Analysis With and Without the Score

Matthew Santa

Texas Tech University

Routledge
Taylor & Francis Group

NEW YORK AND LONDON

First published 2010
by Routledge
270 Madison Ave, New York, NY 10016

Simultaneously published in the UK
by Routledge
2 Park Square, Milton Park, Abingdon, Oxon OX14 4RN

Routledge is an imprint of the Taylor & Francis Group, an informa business

Typeset in ACaslon-Regular by Swales & Willis Ltd, Exeter, Devon
Printed and bound in the United States of America on acid-free paper by
Edwards Brothers, Inc.

Library of Congress Cataloging in Publication Data
Santa, Matthew.
Hearing form : musical analysis with and without the score / Matthew Santa.
    p. cm.
Includes bibliographical references.
1. Musical analysis.   2. Musical form.   I. Title.
MT90.S24 2010
781.8—dc22
                        2009018020

ISBN10: 0–415–87262–6 (set hbk)
ISBN10: 0–415–80091–9 (hbk)
ISBN10: 0–415–87263–4 (set pbk)
ISBN10: 0–415–80092–7 (pbk)
ISBN10: 0–203–86636–3 (set ebk)

ISBN13: 978–0–415–87262–1 (set hbk)
ISBN13: 978–0–415–80091–4 (hbk)
ISBN13: 978–0–415–87263–8 (set pbk)
ISBN13: 978–0–415–80092–1 (pbk)
ISBN13: 978–0–203–86636–8 (set ebk)

for Lisa and Marc

Contents

Preface

As a graduate student, I took a course with Carl Schachter called *Symphonic Works of the Romantic Era*. It was a wonderful class, full of penetrating insights, inspirational discoveries, and also its fair share of good humor (mainly thanks to Schachter's razor-sharp wit). Early on in that class, it was suggested that to best understand a score, you should learn to sing it from memory. Because the course was mostly about Romantic symphonies, to sing any one of the works from memory in its entirety was no small accomplishment—they were all quite long. Though it was never tested or required, nor was the idea even mentioned again after it was initially discussed, I decided to try it. I discovered that much of what I learned about the music from score study could have just as easily been learned without the score, and that, more than anything else, the understanding of musical forms is what made the internalization of these scores possible. This is what led me to write the book that you now have in your hand.

Hearing Form is unique; it is a complete course—textbook/workbook/anthology/music—intended for an upper-level undergraduate college course on the subject of musical forms, or to be used as a supplement to a two- or three-year theory sequence that integrates topics of formal structure with topics of harmony and counterpoint throughout. The first three chapters review topics that are often covered in freshman and sophomore-level courses, while at the same time introducing a style of phrase diagramming and an approach to hearing without the score that is used consistently throughout the book. The goals of this book are to teach students to identify the following with or without a score:

- phrase endings and cadence types in music.
- harmonic sequence types in music.
- modulations in music.
- formal sections in music.
- musical forms.

The Approach

This textbook approaches the topic in as practical a way as possible, and strives to be concise at all times, since often a wealth of information can bury the most important points in a sea of details and exceptions. Some notable characteristics of this book are that it:

- is shaped by recent scholarship, but does not read like a treatise.
- is supported by several unique supplements—its own anthology, a workbook, an instructor's manual and a companion website.
- includes material on popular music and shows how binary, ternary, and variation forms were realized in twentieth-century popular music (blues, jazz, rock, etc.).
- reviews concepts such as score reading, instrumental transposition, cadences, phrase structure, harmonic sequences, and modulation. Courses devoted to musical forms usually require the student to synthesize a vast amount of material learned in earlier coursework, and this text includes the review work necessary in teaching such a course.

Though it is shaped by recent scholarship, this book consciously avoids introducing new terminology specific to the world of music theorists, since few of the terms coined to describe aspects of musical forms in recent years are likely to be adopted and used regularly by the majority of music professionals in the near future. The goal of this book is to teach terminology and concepts that are already in common use by the majority of college-educated professional musicians, and not to introduce terminology found in the latest music theory journals that relate to musical forms. However, in those places where the latest concepts can be introduced without the use of new terminology, this book has done so. (For example, while the term "medial caesura" is never mentioned in the text, the third point under the section on identifying parts of a sonata form without the score reads as follows: "The second theme is often set up by a large cadence on the dominant of either the home key or the secondary key . . . at the end of the bridge, and often this is accompanied by a large rhythmic and textural break.")

The Order of Topics

I benefited greatly from peer reviews while preparing this text for publication. One thing that many of the reviewers suggested I consider changing was the order of topics—more specifically, where to include the chapters on variation forms and imitative forms (currently Chapters 5 and 6). However, of those reviewers who suggested I reconsider the current order, they had different opinions about what sequence of chapters would be best. The suggestions centered around either moving the chapters on variation forms and imitative forms before the chapter on sonata forms (Chapter 4), or moving them after the chapters on concerto forms and rondo forms (Chapters 7 and 8). I believe that the book could be used successfully with the chapters taken in another order, if that is the preference of the instructor. The rationale behind the current ordering is based in part on the literature covered and in part on the pacing of a one-semester course. Finding phrase endings in the literature related to fugue is often difficult for students who are learning to hear phrase endings and cadences with and without the score, and so I wanted the students to grapple with that problem in the context of several other forms first, but many Baroque concerto movements are impossible to understand fully without having studied the structure of a fugue (see p. 90). This suggested to me that imitative forms should be covered later in the book, but should also be covered before concerto forms. While I could have discussed rondo forms immediately after the discussion of sonata forms, I know from personal experience that ending the semester with rondo forms provides a nice summary of earlier topics: it brings the student back to music where phrase endings are easier to find (relative to phrase endings in fugues and some ritornello forms), and it reinforces the importance of sonata form once again by introducing sonata-rondo. Finally, because the rondo principle is itself so simple, it opens up the possibility for reviewing earlier topics in the final weeks of a semester. The pacing of a semester is also the primary reason for placing the chapter on variation forms after sonata form. I spend the first half of the semester on the first five chapters, and the last half of the semester on the last three. "Variation Forms" (Chapter 5) is a fairly easy chapter for students to digest, and so it usually precedes the midterm exam, opening up time for review. It also allows the instructor to start "Imitative Forms" (Chapter 6), possibly the hardest topic for students, after the midterm exam, so that there is plenty of time to spend on the concepts related to imitative forms before the final exam.

Pedagogy

Most of the homework assignments and many of the in-class activities use incomplete phrase diagrams that focus attention on specific details in a piece of music: phrase endings, cadence types, sequence types, key areas, sectional divisions, etc. They also tend to give the students a context for a specific interpretation of that work. One of the main goals in the text is to promote an understanding that there is rarely one and only one "correct" interpretation of a musical work, but this presents a problem to those teaching a form and analysis course. If one allows each student in a class to turn in their own interpretation of a work assigned for homework to a class of ten or more students, then the amount of time it would take to give meaningful feedback to the entire class of students will greatly limit the number of works the class may be assigned, the limit being directly proportional to the number of students in the class. However, incomplete phrase diagrams of a work can be crafted in such a way as to suggest a specific interpretation, which allows one to streamline the grading process considerably.

Very often one musician's phrase is another musician's subphrase, but by indicating the exact location of a phrase ending and how many phrase endings precede it in an incomplete diagram, the student can be directed to respond to a specific interpretation. For example, if there is a primary theme in a sonata form that could reasonably be interpreted as a parallel period with cadences in mm. 4 and 8 or as a parallel double period with cadences in mm. 2, 4, 6, and 8, then an incomplete phrase diagram like this:

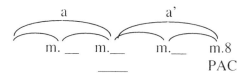

would clearly communicate the two-phrase interpretation to the students as well as focus their attention on identifying the subphrase endings, the first phrase ending, and the cadence type at the end of the first phrase. This kind of approach shifts attention away from choosing between different but equally valid interpretations and onto the *under-standing* of interpretation: how parallel music often demands a parallel interpretation, how sequences, thematic material, and harmonic progressions all influence phrase structure, and how performers communicate a particular interpretation to an audience, to name just a few parts of that understanding. Incomplete phrase diagrams can also be invaluable in allowing students to respond to music without the score; they can calculate measure numbers easily enough if some measure numbers are already given and if they are simply told the meter and whether or not the music starts on a downbeat.

Ancillaries

Workbook

The workbook is bound in the textbook and has perforated pages for the convenience of students and instructors alike. The vast majority of assignments included in the workbook are incomplete phrase diagrams like those discussed above; this approach allows one to cover much more repertoire outside of class than the more traditional method of asking students to prepare an annotated score. Whether the assigned score is two pages or ten pages, the incomplete phrase diagram of it is on just a single workbook page. While it requires the student to listen to and consider the work as a whole just as the annotated score method does, it also has the advantage of providing focus points for student discussions.

Anthology

The choice of selections in the anthology was also based on what is already commonly known by the majority of college-educated professional musicians, without the secondary agenda of bringing the music of under-represented composers to the attention of our students that is seen in most modern music history textbooks. While this secondary agenda is an extremely noble one, there was simply not space in an anthology designed for a one-semester course to include the most commonly performed music and the music of the under-represented in an even-handed way, and so the championing of under-represented composers will be left to the music history textbooks.

All of the works in the anthology are in full score. While some anthologies in the past have chosen to provide piano reductions for larger works, many instructors believe that students need as much practice reading full score as possible. With that in mind, the selections in the anthology are also printed as close to 100 percent of the original printing size as possible, so that the notes will be as easy to read as possible.

The anthology does not include every work discussed in the textbook: because the focus on the text is listening with *and without* the score, many pieces are intended to be studied without the score, and thus are not found in the anthology. This includes all of the popular music from the twentieth century that is discussed in the textbook, as well as a handful of other pieces. Post-tonal music is not discussed in the textbook at all, and thus is not covered in the anthology. Audio tracks for the anthology are licenced from Naxos of America, Inc. Access is through the book's companion website, described below.

Instructor's Manual

An instructor's manual on CD-ROM is provided upon request to instructors. It is divided into four parts: 1) a section on teaching strategies; 2) a quiz bank; 3) a test bank; and 4) a guide to all of the homework assignments in the workbook. To my knowledge, no other form and analysis textbooks have a workbook or instructor's manual, though many instructors value their use in courses on harmony.

Companion Website

A companion website for students and instructors houses audio tracks and supplementary materials for the course, including recordings for all of the pieces in the *Anthology for Hearing Form*, by permission of Naxos of America, Inc. These are accessible under password protection for students taking the course, and available to download at no additional charge. The website also hosts sample quizzes, supplementary assignments, and scores not included in the anthology, as well as information for instructors to request the instructor's manual discussed above.

The web address is: www.routledge.com/textbooks/9780415872638

Acknowledgments

I wish to thank all of my friends and colleagues whose support, advice, editorial comments, and generous criticisms helped to shape this book. Jeannie Barrick, Michael Berry, Andrew Davis, Peter Martens, and Michael Stoune read all or part of the manuscript and made many valuable suggestions. I am deeply grateful to all of them and hope that they will be pleased with the shape that this book has ultimately taken. Many thanks also go to Walter Meyer and Thomas Cimarusti for providing their translations of songs in foreign languages; to James Greeson, who generously allowed me to use the scores that he made available online for his own students; to Richard Willis, who provided a great deal of expert editorial assistance at the end of this project; and to those who helped me prepare the scores for the anthology—Nicholas Dragga, Justin Houser, Brian Moseley, John Pekowski, Charles Richard Santa, and Bryant Smith. The book is also considerably better for the tireless efforts and boundless energy of those at Routledge who worked on the project, especially Constance Ditzel; I sincerely thank her and all of her coworkers for their time and support. My special thanks go to my wife, Lisa Garner Santa, whose love and support served as an inspiration throughout, and whose exemplary musicianship served as a guiding light. This book is dedicated to her and to my son, Marc.

chapter 1

Cadences and Phrases

There are few things as fundamental to crafting an artistic musical performance as shaping a phrase through subtle nuances in dynamics, rhythm, and articulation. However, shaping a phrase depends upon one's knowledge of phrases and cadences; one can only shape phrases if one knows how to find where phrases begin and end, and how cadences are used to mark phrase endings. This chapter will focus on phrases and cadences, as well as on other elements that are essential to analyzing phrase structure.

Cadences

Cadences are gestures that serve to end a musical idea. Usually many different aspects of the music contribute to a cadence: melody, harmony, rhythm, dynamics, articulation, phrasing, vocal text, and ornamentation can all contribute to a cadence's sense of closure. While all of these aspects can play a role, cadences are generally categorized by harmonic progression, and can be understood in terms of four basic types: *authentic*, *half*, *plagal*, and *deceptive*.

Authentic cadences have the harmonic progression $V^{(7)}$–I ($V^{(7)}$–i in minor), and can be divided further into two subcategories: perfect and imperfect. Authentic cadences are **perfect** if they have both of the following characteristics:

1   Both chords are in root position (i.e. the bass line is "so-do").

2   The tonic pitch is in the main melodic voice of the final I chord.

If the authentic cadence does not have both of these characteristics, then it is considered **imperfect**. Haydn's St. Anthony Chorale (the theme of *Variations on a Theme by Haydn*, by Brahms) provides an example of both types (for full score, see Anthology, pp. 116–17):

EXAMPLE 1.1   Brahms, *Variations on a Theme by Haydn*, mm. 6–14.

In the motion from m. 9 to m. 10, there is a perfect authentic cadence: V and I, F and B♭, are both in root position, and the tonic is found in the main melodic voice of the final I chord. In the motion from m. 13 to m. 14, there is an imperfect authentic cadence: the third is in the soprano voice of the final tonic chord. (While V chords are also implied in mm. 10 and 14, these are more like harmonized embellishments of the larger harmonic motion from downbeat to downbeat in each case.)

Finally, one should note that vii°⁽⁷⁾–I (vii°⁽⁷⁾–i in minor) is also considered to be an imperfect authentic cadence, because the progression is a harmonic substitution for V⁽⁷⁾–I (some musicians refer to this as a leading-tone cadence).

Half cadences are two-chord harmonic progressions that end on a V⁽⁷⁾ chord (the first chord can be anything). The first eight measures of Beethoven's Piano Sonata No. 1 end with a strong half cadence:

EXAMPLE 1.2   Beethoven, Piano Sonata No. 1, mm. 5–8.

One type of half cadence has been given a special name: the progression iv⁶–V in minor is called a Phrygian half cadence (the cadence is called "Phrygian" because cadences with a descending half step in the bass are commonly associated with music based on the

Phrygian mode). Such a cadence ends the second vocal phrase of Purcell's famous aria "When I Am Laid in Earth" (for full score, see Anthology, p. 373):

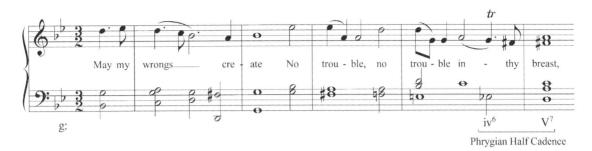

EXAMPLE 1.3 Purcell, *Dido and Aeneas*, "When I Am Laid in Earth," mm. 10–14.

Note how a trill embellishes the penultimate chord of the cadence; this is one way that composers mark all kinds of cadences for the listener, especially in Baroque music.

Occasionally, one will hear a cadential progression ending with vii°(7); this is also considered a half cadence, since vii° is a harmonic substitute for V.

Plagal cadences have the harmonic progression IV–I (iv–i in minor). The final cadence of Handel's "Hallelujah Chorus" from *Messiah* is a famous example:

EXAMPLE 1.4 Handel, *Messiah*, "Hallelujah Chorus," mm. 90–94.

The cadential progression ii$_5^6$–I (ii°$_5^6$–i in minor) is also considered to be a plagal cadence, as it is a harmonic substitution for IV–I (in which case ii$_5^6$ is really functioning as IV^{add6}).

Deceptive cadences have the harmonic motion V–vi (V–VI in minor). In Handel's instrumental introduction to the aria "Non disperar" in *Giulio Cesare*, a deceptive cadence in m. 8 sets up a more final cadential gesture in m. 9 (for full score, see Anthology, p. 220):

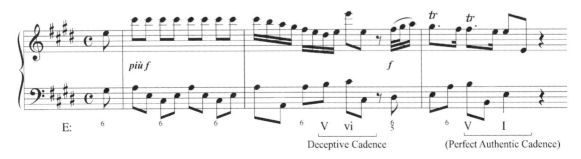

EXAMPLE 1.5 Handel, *Giulio Cesare*, "Non disperar," mm. 7–9.

Deceptive cadences almost always require a follow-up cadence that is more conclusive, just as this one did.

The cadential progression V–IV⁶ (V–iv⁶ in minor) is also considered to be a deceptive cadence, as it is a harmonic substitution for V–vi. In either progression, the bass line motion is "so-la" where one is expecting "so-do."

Cadences are often referred to by their standard abbreviations:

PAC = Perfect Authentic Cadence
IAC = Imperfect Authentic Cadence
HC = Half Cadence
PC = Plagal Cadence
DC = Deceptive Cadence

Some types of cadences are stronger than others, and while relative strengths vary greatly within each type, the diagram below helps to illustrate a widely accepted generalization:

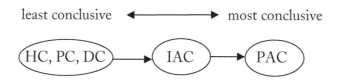

How to Identify Cadence Types When Listening Without the Score

1   Always be sure to orient yourself tonally by singing through a tonic triad.

2   Ascending half steps in the main melodic voice usually signal authentic cadences. Try singing or thinking along with the solfege syllables "ti-do" when you hear one at a cadence point. Although "ti-do" could also be harmonized by a deceptive cadence, authentic cadences are by far more common and the sound of "being deceived" is usually pretty obvious, so you should have little trouble choosing between the two.

3   Descending half steps in the main melodic voice usually signal half cadences. Try singing or thinking along with the solfege syllables "do-ti" when you hear one at a cadence point. If it fits, then it is a half cadence.

4   Any cadence ending on "re" in the main melodic voice is a half cadence, while most cadences ending on "do" or "mi" are authentic cadences.

5   The bass line is almost always useful in hearing a cadence. While perfect fifths are common in tonal music, you should be able to pick out the fifth that is "so-do" if you have properly oriented yourself. The bass line "so-do" at a cadence point signals an authentic cadence, while the bass line "do-so" at a cadence point signals a half cadence. The bass line "so-so-do" signals an authentic cadence with an embellished V chord (often embellished with a cadential $^6_4$).

6   Any cadence ending on "la" in the bass is a deceptive cadence.

7   Use your knowledge of what is common to guide your hearing. Authentic cadences are the most common type, so first consider that as a possibility. Half cadences are the second most common type of cadence, so consider that as a possibility second.

In-Class Activity 1.1

Identify the cadences in mm. 4, 8, 12, 16, and 18 of Mozart's Piano Sonata, K. 331, I *without the score* (it's in 6/8, so you don't need the score to use these measure numbers—just keep conduct and track of downbeats while listening and note that mm. 1–8 repeat). Listen to it at least two times, and pause the music at cadence points on the last hearing.

In More Detail: Progressive and Conclusive Cadences

Occasionally, one will find a cadence that does not fit the definitions for any of the four cadence types mentioned in this chapter so far. In discussing such cadences, some musicians use a more general pair of terms: *progressive cadences* and *conclusive cadences*. **Progressive cadences** (sometimes called *incomplete cadences*) are cadences that do not end on a tonic, while **conclusive cadences** (sometimes called *complete cadences*) are cadences that do end on the tonic. The opening to Mozart's Symphony No. 40 provides an excellent example of a progressive cadence (for full score, see Anthology, p. 315).

EXAMPLE 1.6   Mozart, Symphony No. 40, I, mm. 1–5.

In m. 5, the first phrase ends on a $ii^{\circ 4}_2$ chord, and can thus not be understood as any of the more common cadence types. However, the label "progressive" adequately describes its relationship to the next phrase, which ends in an IAC.

Note that the labels "progressive cadence" or "conclusive cadence" should not be used to describe a cadence if a more specific label is appropriate (those being HC, IAC, PAC, PC, and DC); they should only be used if none of the more specific labels fit. It is also interesting to note that this more general pair of terms begs the question of whether or not plagal cadences deserve to be heard as more conclusive than the diagram on p. 4 (where plagal cadences are grouped with half cadences and deceptive cadences) suggests. After all, plagal cadences do end on the tonic, unlike the other two cadences in the "least conclusive" category.

Motives and Phrases

A **motive** is a short melodic and/or rhythmic idea, while a **phrase** is an independent musical idea terminated by a cadence. Motives are the building blocks of phrases. While motives don't depend on harmony for their definition, phrases do: phrases must have at least one cadential change of harmony to define their ending. Consider the first phrase of Beethoven's 5th Symphony (for full score, see Anthology, pp. 97–98):

EXAMPLE 1.7   Beethoven, Symphony No. 5, I, mm. 6–21.

The first four notes constitute the motive upon which the rest of the first movement is based: short-short-short-long starting on an upbeat could characterize the rhythm of the motive, while three repetitions of the same note followed by a descending third leap could characterize its melodic shape. It is heard eleven times in the first phrase (see brackets), though in several subtle variations. The first phrase, however, does not end until m. 21, when there is a sufficiently strong harmonic change to signal a cadence.

Music teachers often tell their students that they must find the peak of the phrase in order to shape it correctly, but that requires the students to know where the phrases are. Good musicians avoid making decisions about phrasing based solely on the melody, since this commonly leads to misinterpreting motives and subphrases as phrases. Phrase endings are defined by the interaction of the bass line, the top line, and the inner voices, and so one must pay close attention to the harmonic progression when making decisions about phrasing. Now, consider the first phrase of Beethoven's First Piano Sonata (see opposite):

The first melodic idea ends in m. 2, but there is no harmonic change in those measures and so, while they certainly create an independent musical idea, they would be better described as the first half of a phrase (it is too long to be called a motive). One could argue that mm. 1–8 constitute a single phrase, but one could also reasonably argue that mm. 1–8 actually constitute two four-bar phrases, and there is no single right answer. There is a great amount of subjectivity in phrasing, which can be viewed either as invigorating or as frustrating. Such flexibility is one of the things that allows a musician to personalize their performance, and thus is one of the things that can mark an individual artist's interpretation of a musical work.

A **subphrase** is a musical idea that sounds independent melodically, but not harmonically, and that can be understood as part of a phrase (e.g. mm. 1–2 of the Beethoven

EXAMPLE 1.8   Beethoven, Piano Sonata Op. 2, No. 1, I, mm. 1–8.

Sonata above). Consider the opening to the Badinerie from Bach's Orchestral Suite No. 2 (for full score, see Anthology, p. 13):

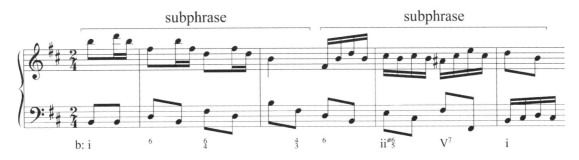

EXAMPLE 1.9   Bach, Orchestral Suite No. 2, Badinerie, mm. 1–4.

The quarter note in m. 2 of the flute part communicates a strong melodic closure, but there has been no harmonic change. The phrase ending is in m. 4, but the strong melodic closure halfway through divides the phrase evenly into two subphrases.

In More Detail: Symmetrical Phrasing

Symmetrical phrasing (sometimes called *regular phrasing*) can mean two different things: either a single phrase is divided into two subphrases of the same length, or a group of phrases is divided into two phrases of the same length (the most common case is a pair of four-measure phrases). Symmetrical phrasing is considered a style-defining feature of Classical period music, but is very common in other periods and styles as well. The opening to Mozart's Piano Sonata, K. 331 illustrates this:

EXAMPLE 1.10   Mozart, Piano Sonata, K. 331, I, mm. 1–8.

Conversely, **Asymmetrical phrasing** (sometimes called *irregular phrasing*) means that either a single phrase is divided into two subphrases of different lengths, or a group of phrases is divided into two phrases of different lengths. Though irregular phrases can be found in Classical period music, they are the exception that proves the rule. They can be found more easily in music from the Baroque period or the Romantic period, though regular phrases are still more common overall. The opening of the St. Anthony Chorale is an example of asymmetrical phrasing:

EXAMPLE 1.11   Brahms, *Variations on a Theme by Haydn*, mm. 1–10.

One could interpret the bracketed units as phrases or as subphrases (there are harmonic motions from V to vi in mm. 3 and 8); either way, it is asymmetrical.

A **phrase diagram** is meant to capture one's interpretation of a particular musical form. Compare the music in Example 1.12 to the phrase diagram that follows it.

Slurs are used to represent phrases. Each slur is labeled with a letter that marks both where that phrase occurs in the music and how its melodic material relates to the phrases that came before it. One adds lower-case letters to each successive phrase (a, b, c, etc.), using a new letter for each phrase that sounds truly independent of those that came before it. If a phrase is an exact or almost exact repetition of an earlier phrase, one uses the earlier letter associated with that material; if it sounds like an altered version of an earlier phrase, one uses the earlier letter associated with that material and adds either a number (a1, a2, etc.) or a prime symbol (a, a′, a″, etc.) to indicate the variation.

EXAMPLE 1.12 J. S. Bach, *Notebook for Anna Magdalena Bach*, "March," and accompanying phrase diagram.

How phrases are labeled with letters in a phrase diagram can be highly subjective, and so can decisions about the number of phrases in a passage of music, but the process of doing so is nevertheless very useful, as it reveals more about your potential choices in the interpretation of a musical work. Consider the first section of the Air from Bach's Orchestral Suite No. 3 (for full score, see Anthology, pp. 14–15):

EXAMPLE 1.13   J. S. Bach, Orchestral Suite No. 3, Air, mm. 1–6.

One could diagram this section in a number of different ways, but each way would reflect a different interpretation, and the differences in some cases would also reflect different performance choices (in particular, interpretations that differed in the number of phrases would certainly reflect subtly different performances). Below are the most viable possibilities:

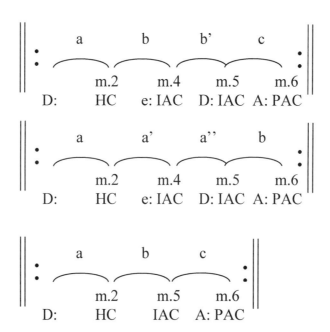

Note: It's important to note that the measure numbers in a phrase diagram indicate where the *last note* of each phrase occurs.

Notice that the first four interpretations assert that the last phrase of the section begins with the same note that ends the previous phrase. This is called an **elision**, and is especially common in Baroque music. The elision is represented in the diagram by the way the beginning of the last slur overlaps the end of the previous one. (One should also note that the cadence in m. 4 is not truly a modulation to E minor, but merely a tonicization.) One might initially gravitate toward the first two choices, but the latter three are based on a deeper harmonic understanding: there is a descending fifths sequence in mm. 3–5, a patterned progression of chord roots—F♯–B–E–A–D—that undercuts the phrase boundaries that are suggested by the melody (see the circled notes in the score; sequence types will be discussed in the next section). To better account for this conflict between melodic cues and harmonic ones, one could add more detail to the last choice provided above and interpret the phrases of the first choice as subphrases in the last choice, like so:

Note: While both phrases and subphrases are diagrammed with slurs, one can easily distinguish between the two, because subphrases occur underneath larger slurs, while phrases do not.

The other interpretations are not wrong, just different, but one must consider the merits of each in order to make an informed choice as a performer.

Sequences

Musical sequences often shape how we hear phrasing. A **melodic sequence** is a patterned series of transpositions of the same melodic fragment in a single voice or part. A **harmonic sequence** is a patterned progression of chord roots (down by fifth, up by step, etc.);

a harmonic sequence is often accompanied by a melodic sequence in one or more voices. The sequence in mm. 3–5 of Bach's Air is both melodic and harmonic: the melodic sequence transposes melodic material every four beats, while the harmonic sequence changes chords every two beats (the bass notes on beat 2 of each measure are passing tones).

One fundamental rule of musical interpretation is that a sequence must be handled like a vehicle that takes the listener somewhere; it is undesirable to create a musical break such as a phrase ending that contradicts the flow of a sequence. For example, the interpretations of Bach's Air only acknowledged phrase beginnings and endings that were synchronized with the internal transpositions and changes of the sequence. Each was consistent with itself— that is, if the sequence was broken into phrases, then there was a cadence at the end of each part of the melodic sequence, but if the whole sequence was heard as part of a larger phrase, then each part of the sequence was interpreted as a subphrase. Conversely, it would be unmusical to suggest an interpretation that acknowledges a cadence in m. 4, but no cadence in m. 5.

While musicians generally do not specify the interval of transposition in identifying melodic sequences, they often identify harmonic sequences according to the size and direction of the intervallic motions from chord root to chord root. There are just six types: ascending and descending step sequences, ascending and descending third sequences, and ascending and descending fifth sequences. This labeling system assumes octave equivalence, so the literal intervals in the bass line are not important: a descending fifth motion is considered the same as an ascending fourth, a descending third the same as an ascending sixth, and so on. By convention, harmonic sequences are labeled by steps, thirds, and fifths, and not by fourths, sixths, and sevenths.

Of all the sequence types, descending fifth sequences are by far the most common in tonal music. The first movement of Mozart's Symphony No. 40 provides a particularly clear example of this sequence (F–B♭–E♭–A♭–D–G) (for full score, see Anthology, p. 327):

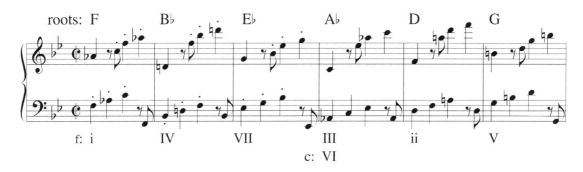

EXAMPLE 1.14   Mozart, Symphony No. 40, I, mm. 202–208.

Notice that not all of the fourths and fifths in this descending fifth sequence are perfect: the motion from A♭ to D is an augmented fourth. This is commonplace; the quality of the intervals in any sequence can vary without any real consequence to its definition. What defines a sequence type is the size of the intervals involved and not their quality.

While ascending and descending fifth sequences involve moving by fourth or fifth with every change in chord root, ascending and descending step and third sequences often alternate between two different types of root motions (second/seventh, third/sixth, and fourth/fifth are the three general types of root motions). For example, one of the most common types of descending third sequences is realized as a regular alternation between descending fourths and ascending steps, as in Pachelbel's Canon:

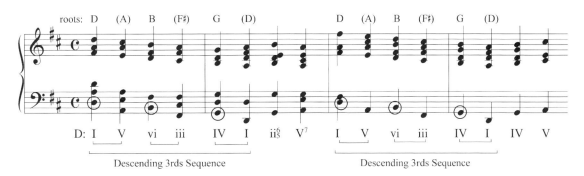

EXAMPLE 1.15   Johann Pachelbel, Canon in D, mm. 1–4.

The combination of a descending fourth and an ascending step yields a total motion of a descending third, and so the sequence is labeled accordingly. In general, sequences with a regular alternation between two types of root motions are labeled by the overall motion when the two different types of root motions are combined (e.g. an alternation between ascending fourths and descending thirds yields an ascending step sequence, an alternation between ascending thirds and descending steps yields an ascending step sequence, etc.). The first movement of Haydn's Symphony No. 103 provides another example of a descending thirds sequence (note that this example is a melodic sequence as well as a harmonic one) (for full score, see Anthology, p. 261):

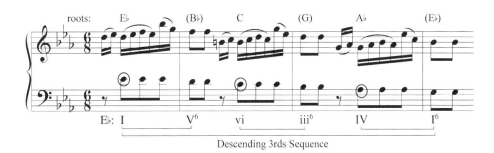

EXAMPLE 1.16   Haydn, Symphony No. 103, I, mm. 51–54.

How to Identify Harmonic Sequences When Listening Without the Score

1   Always be sure to orient yourself tonally by finding the tonic and singing through a tonic triad.
2   First sing the bass line along with the music, paying close attention to whether or not each bass note sounds like a chord root or like some other note of the chord. Then try singing the chord roots along with the music. Then sing it back to yourself and identify the intervals that you are singing.

3 Use your knowledge of what is common to guide your hearing: descending fifth sequences are the most common type, followed by descending third sequences, ascending step sequences, and ascending fifth sequences.

4 Learn which bass lines are associated with the most common types of sequences.

5 Descending fifth sequences are most commonly realized with one of the following four bass lines: a) a chain of descending fifths and ascending fourths (so that the larger motion is a descending step every two chords); b) with every other chord in inversion, a chain of descending thirds and ascending steps (so that the larger motion is a descending step every two chords); c) with every chord in inversion, a chain of descending steps and repeated notes (so that the larger motion is a descending step every two chords); d) with every chord in inversion and every other chord a secondary dominant, a chromatically descending bass line.

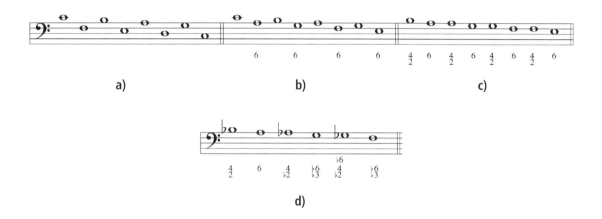

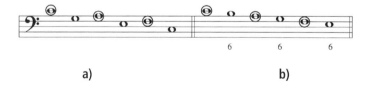

6 Descending third sequences are most commonly realized with one of the following two bass lines: a) a chain of descending fourths and ascending steps (so that the larger motion is a descending third every two chords); b) with every other chord in inversion, a descending stepwise bass line.

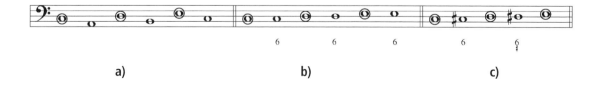

7 Ascending step sequences are most commonly realized with one of the following three bass lines: a) a chain of descending thirds and ascending fourths (so that the larger motion is an ascending step every two chords); b) with every other chord in inversion, a chain of repeated notes and ascending steps (so that the larger motion is an ascending step every two chords); c) with every other chord a secondary dominant in inversion, a chromatically ascending bass line.

8 Ascending fifth sequences are most commonly realized with a bass line that is a chain of ascending fifths and descending fourths (so that the larger motion is an ascending step every two chords). Because a regular alternation between fourths and fifths is also commonly used to realize descending fifth sequences, you benefit greatly by paying attention to the overall motion (either a stepwise descent or a stepwise ascent).

In-Class Activity 1.2

Diagram the phrase structure of the Air from J. S. Bach's Orchestral Suite No. 3 in D major (see Anthology, pp. 14–15). The first part has already been discussed, but choose an interpretation of it and then diagram the second half. Be sure to label any harmonic sequences you find by type (↓5th seq., ↓3rd seq., etc.).

Homework Assignment 1.1

Listen to the theme (marked "Aria" in the score) from J. S. Bach's Goldberg Variations while following along with the score (see Anthology, p. 1), and mark cadence points in the score as you listen. Then look at Homework Assignment 1.1 in your workbook, choose the incomplete phrase diagram that most closely matches the number of cadences you heard, and fill in the blanks of that diagram with cadence types, sequence types, measure numbers or key areas, as appropriate (blanks after arrows are for keys). Next, look at the incomplete phrase diagram that did not reflect your initial hearing, and fill in the blanks of that diagram. Finally, listen again while following this latter diagram and see if you can understand the logic behind the other interpretation.

Cadential Extensions and Links

Not all melodic material in a composition can be understood as part of a phrase. Melodic gestures that do not seem independent, but that are separated from the melodic material both before and after them by strong phrase endings and phrase beginnings, are better understood in terms of *cadential extensions* and *links*.

A **cadential extension** serves to bring the preceding phrase to a satisfying close, and is thus dependent upon it. The cadential extension could provide an additional cadence that is more satisfying than the previous one, or merely extend the final cadence of the previous phrase by adding figuration or by simply sustaining the notes of the final cadential chord. Consider this passage from Brahms' *Variations on a Theme by Haydn* (for full score, see Anthology, p. 117):

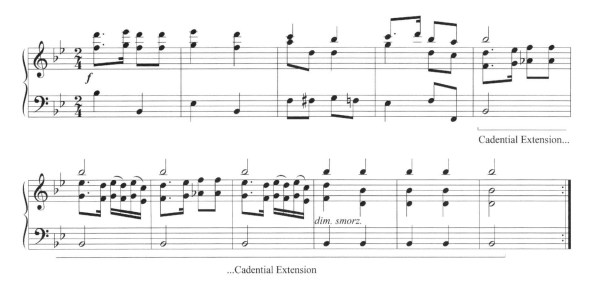

EXAMPLE 1.17   Brahms, *Variations on a Theme by Haydn*, mm. 23–29.

Deceptive cadences almost demand cadential extensions. Consider this cadential extension in Handel's music (for full score, see Anthology, p. 220):

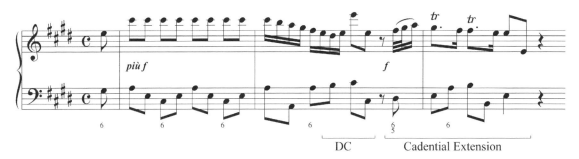

EXAMPLE 1.18   Handel, *Giulio Cesare*, "Non disperar," mm. 7–9.

A **link** is music that serves as a bridge between two phrases, and is dependent upon what comes both before and after it for its definition. A link joins the first two sections in the first movement of Mozart's Symphony No. 40 (for full score, see Anthology, pp. 320–321):

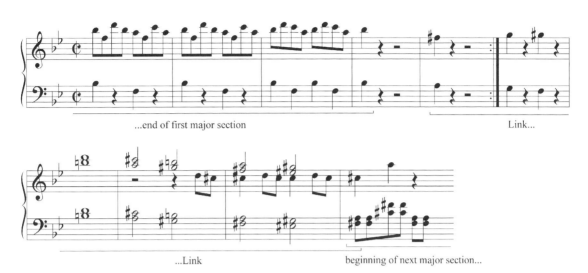

...end of first major section

Link...

...Link

beginning of next major section...

EXAMPLE 1.19   Mozart, Symphony No. 40, I, mm. 96–105.

Cadential extensions and links will be diagrammed at the phrase level just like phrases, but will be differentiated from phrases because they will not be given phrase labels (i.e. "a, b, a′," etc.). Instead they should be labeled as "cad. ext." or "link," respectively.

$$
\begin{array}{cccc}
\text{a} & \text{link} & \text{b} & \\
\text{(m.95)} & \text{m.99} & \text{m.105} & \text{(m.107)} \\
\text{B}\flat: & \text{PAC} & \text{f}\sharp: &
\end{array}
$$

EXAMPLE 1.20   Phrase diagram of Mozart, Symphony No. 40, mm. 96–105.

Cadential extensions and links may or may not end with a new cadence; the interpretation shown above does not take a new cadence where the link joins the first phrase of the next section. The cadential extension in Example 1.17 doesn't end with a cadence either, since that extension merely prolongs the tonic chord that began in m. 27. The cadential extension in Example 1.18, however, definitely ends with a new cadence; the PAC at the end of that example is needed to bring balance after the deceptive cadence in m. 8.

In-Class Activity 1.3

Complete a phrase diagram of the theme from Mozart's Piano Sonata, K. 331, I *without the score* (use the cadences you identified in Activity 1.1). Then compare your hearing to the score. How would describe the melodic material at the end of the theme?

In-Class Activity 1.4

Identify cadences in the theme from Brahm's *Variations on a Theme by Haydn* without the score (it's in 2/4, so you don't need the score to use measure numbers—just conduct and keep track of downbeats while listening). Listen to it at least two times, and pause the music at cadence points on the last hearing. Then complete a phrase diagram of the theme. Finally, compare your hearing to the score.

Homework Assignment 1.2

Look at Homework Assignment 1.2 in your workbook, and listen to Schubert's "Kennst du das Land?" (*Mignon*, D. 321) without the score while conducting along in 2/4. Use the steady meter and measure numbers to follow along with the diagram. Then fill in the blanks of the diagram with cadence types, measure numbers or key areas, as appropriate, and answer the questions at the bottom of the page. Finally, listen again while following the diagram and see if you can understand the logic behind the interpretive choices that differed from your own.

Homework Assignment 1.3

Choose an art song from the Baroque, Classical, or Romantic period that is not included in the Anthology and analyze its phrase structure, key areas, and harmonic sequences by preparing an annotated score. To show its phrase structure, mark each phrase ending where it occurs with the cadence type below the system and each subphrase ending with a comma above the system. Also, label key areas and harmonic sequences (by type) where they occur.

Homework Assignment 1.4

Choose a movement from a Baroque, Classical, or Romantic-period choral work or instrumental chamber work that is not included in the Anthology and analyze its phrase structure, key areas, and harmonic sequences by preparing an annotated score. To show its phrase structure, mark each phrase ending where it occurs with the cadence type below the system and each subphrase ending with a comma above the system. Also, label key areas and harmonic sequences (by type) where they occur.

Homework Assignment 1.5

Write a 1–2 page essay comparing cadences and phrase structure in music with punctuation and sentence structure in English.

Chapter Review

1 A **cadence** is a musical gesture that serves to end an idea. There are four common types of cadences: **authentic** cadences (V–I), **half** cadences (ending on V), **plagal** cadences (IV–I), and **deceptive** cadences (V–vi). Authentic cadences are further divided into two subcategories: **perfect**, in which the V–I motion is realized with both chords in root position, and with scale-degree 1 in the main melodic voice of the tonic chord, and **imperfect**, in which one or both of those conditions is not met.

2 In a phrase diagram, cadences are distinguished by one of the following abbreviations: IAC, PAC, HC, PC, and DC. It's important to note that the measure numbers in a phrase diagram indicate where the *last note* of each phrase occurs.

3 Certain harmonic substitutions at cadence points are common enough to warrant memorization: vii° can substitute for V in an authentic cadence or a half cadence, ii$_5^6$ can substitute for IV in a plagal cadence (in which case ii$_5^6$ is really functioning as IV^{add6}), and IV^6 can substitute for vi in a deceptive cadence.

4 A **motive** is a short musical idea. A **phrase** is an independent musical idea terminated by a cadence. Motives are the building blocks of phrases.

5 A **subphrase** is a musical idea that sounds independent melodically, but not harmonically, and that can be understood as part of a phrase. In a phrase diagram, a phrase is represented by a slur, while a subphrase is represented by a slur underneath a larger slur. Phrases are labeled with letters (a, b, c, etc.), while subphrases are not.

6 An **elision** is a joining together of two phrases, such that the second phrase begins with the same note that ends the first phrase.

7 A **melodic sequence** is a patterned series of transpositions of the same melodic fragment in a single voice or part. A **harmonic sequence** is a patterned progression of chord roots (down by fifth, up by step, etc.); a harmonic sequence is often accompanied by a melodic sequence in one or more voices.

8 Harmonic sequences fall into one of six categories: ascending fifth sequences, descending fifth sequences, ascending third sequences, descending third sequences, ascending step sequences, and descending step sequences. Sequences with a regular alternation between two types of root motions are labeled by the overall motion when the two different types of root motions are combined (e.g. a fourth down alternating with a step up combines to form a *descending third sequence*).

9 A **cadential extension** is music that serves to bring the preceding phrase to a satisfying close, and is thus dependent upon it. In a phrase diagram, cadential extensions are represented by slurs and labeled "cad. ext."

10 A **link** is music that serves as a bridge between two phrases, and is dependent upon what comes both before and after it for its definition. In a phrase diagram, links are represented by slurs and labeled "link."

chapter 2

Phrase Organization

One characteristic of memorable melodies is that their phrases often group together in ways that make the melody seem both well-balanced and complete in itself. While the last chapter explored phrases and cadences, this chapter will focus on the different ways in which phrases can be grouped together.

Periods and Phrase Groups

A **period** is a pair of phrases in which the second phrase ends with a more conclusive cadence than the first. Within the pair, the first phrase is called the **antecedent** and the second phrase is called the **consequent**. A **phrase group** is a group of two or more phrases that seem to belong together, but don't form a period because the final cadence of the group is *not* more conclusive than the first. (Because the definition of a period is dependent upon the relative conclusiveness of its cadences, one should memorize the diagram of cadences and their relative strengths on p. 4.)

Periods may be either parallel or contrasting. In a **parallel period**, the second phrase begins with material from the first phrase, while in a **contrasting period**, the second phrase doesn't. Example 2.1 illustrates a parallel period in the music of Brahms (for full

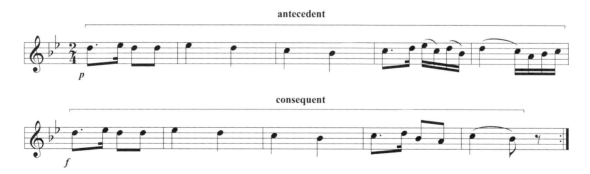

EXAMPLE 2.1   Brahms, *Variations on a Theme by Haydn*, mm. 1–10.

score, see Anthology, p. 116), while Example 2.2 illustrates a contrasting period in the music of Beethoven:

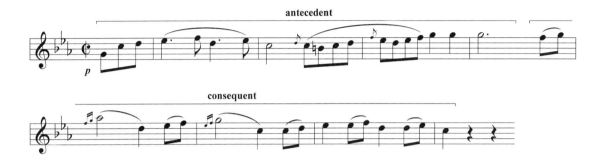

EXAMPLE 2.2   Beethoven, Piano Sonata, Op. 13 (Pathétique), III, mm. 1–8.

While the definition of a period depends upon the relative strength of its two cadences, it does not depend upon those cadences being in the same key; thus, it is possible to have a **modulating period**, in which the second cadence is a more conclusive cadence type than the first, but is in a different key. Example 2.3 illustrates the modulating period that begins the third movement of Haydn's Piano Sonata No. 37.

EXAMPLE 2.3   Haydn, Piano Sonata No. 37, III, mm. 1–8.

A **double period** is a group of four phrases presented as two pairs in which the second pair ends with a more conclusive cadence than the first pair. Example 2.4 illustrates the double period that begins Beethoven's Piano Sonata, Op. 26, I.

It is important to remember that a double period *will not necessarily be made up of two periods*, as the name seems to imply. In the Example 2.4, the first pair of phrases do not form a period, though the second one does. It is called a double period because it is *twice the length* of a period, not because it is composed of two periods. One should also note that double periods are usually parallel (i.e. each pair of phrases in a double period usually begins with the same material).

EXAMPLE 2.4   Beethoven, Piano Sonata, Op. 26, I, mm. 1–16.

In-Class Activity 2.1

Diagram the phrase structure of mm. 44–66 in Mozart's Symphony No. 40, I, and identify the phrase organization without the score. Listen to it twice. After the first hearing, identify the number of phrases. After the second, identify the cadence types and phrase structure.

In-Class Activity 2.2

Diagram the phrase structure of mm. 1–16 in Haydn's Piano Sonata No. 33, Hob. XVI: 20, I, and identify the phrase organization without the score. Listen to it twice. After the first hearing, identify the number of phrases. After the second, identify the cadence types and phrase structure.

Homework Assignment 2.1

Diagram the phrase structure of mm. 40–48 and mm. 80–94 in Haydn's Symphony No. 103, I, and identify the phrase organization.

In-Class Activity 2.3

Diagram the phrase structure of mm. 45–57 in Beethoven's Symphony No. 3, I, and identify the phrase organization without the score. Listen to it twice. After the first hearing, identify the number of phrases. After the second, identify the cadence types and phrase structure.

Homework Assignment 2.2

Diagram the phrase structure of mm. 1–20 and mm. 38–53 in Mozart's Symphony No. 35, IV, and identify the phrase organization.

Three-Phrase Periods and Repetition Within a Period

Though periods are typically defined in terms of two phrases, one can easily expand the concept to explain groups of three distinct phrases in which the final cadence is stronger than the first and at least as strong as the second, and one can also use the term to describe larger groups of phrases that can be understood as periods with internal repetition. The following examples show the three-phrase period that begins Mozart's Piano Sonata, K. 332, and the contrasting period with internal repetition that begins the third movement of Beethoven's Piano Sonata, Op. 13 (Pathétique):

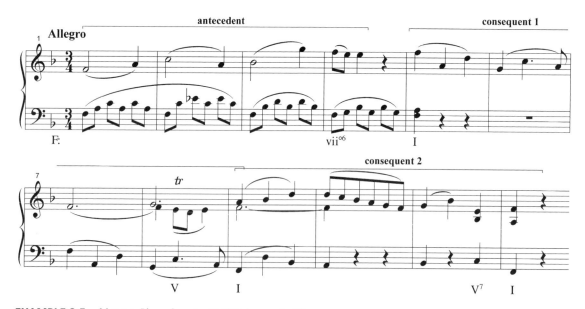

EXAMPLE 2.5   Mozart, Piano Sonata, K. 332, I, mm. 1–12.

EXAMPLE 2.6 Beethoven, Piano Sonata, Op. 13, III, mm. 1–17.

In this last example, both the repetition of the consequent phrase and the repetition of the cadential extension are varied repetitions, but in neither case would the variation cause the listener to mistake the repetition of material for new material.

Sentences

A **sentence** is a pair of phrases or subphrases that consists of a four-measure **presentation** followed by a four-measure **continuation**. In the presentation, a basic idea is presented and

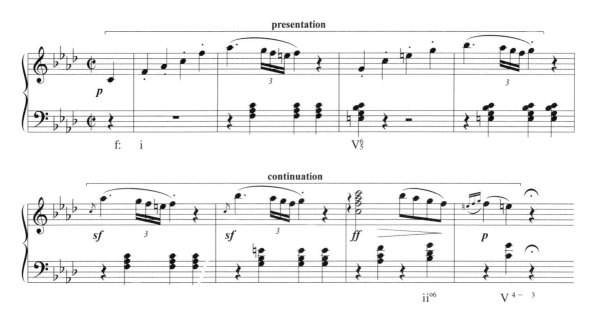

EXAMPLE 2.7   Beethoven, Piano Sonata No. 1, mm. 1–8.

then repeated, with the repetition often varied to outline a different harmony. In the continuation, a motive from the basic idea is developed, and then that development is followed by a cadential gesture that brings the sentence to a close. The archetypical example is the first eight measures from Beethoven's First Piano Sonata.

The primary difference between a period and a sentence is tied to how the two halves of each relate to one another. In a period, the consequent phrase sounds more like an independent unit and its cadence must be more conclusive than the one ending the antecedent phrase. In a sentence, the continuation might be independent enough to be considered a phrase in its own right, but it might not (in which case, it would be considered a subphrase). In a sentence, the second half (continuation) sounds more like a development of material from the first half (presentation).

The proportions of a sentence are also important to its definition: the presentation is divided into 2 + 2, and the continuation is divided into 1 + 1 + 2, as is illustrated in Example 2.8a. These proportions can be expanded, as long as the expanded form is simply a multiple of the smaller one; for example, a 4 + 4 presentation followed by a 2 + 2 + 4 continuation, as shown in Example 2.8b.

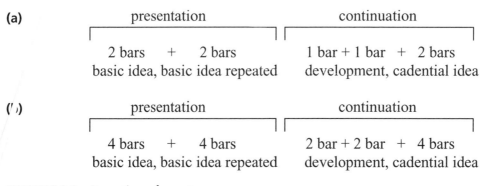

EXAMPLE 2.8   Proportions of a sentence.

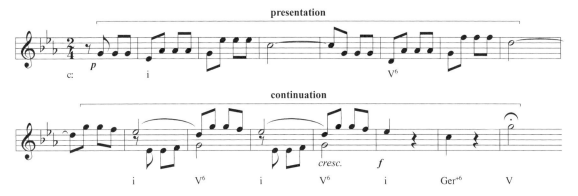

EXAMPLE 2.9 Beethoven Symphony No. 5, I, mm. 6–21.

These same proportions are found in the first theme from Beethoven's 5th Symphony (for full score, see Anthology, pp. 97–98).

After a short five-bar introduction in which the familiar four-note motive is presented, a 16-bar unit is presented that can easily be broken down into an 8-bar presentation (4 + 4), and an 8-bar continuation (2 + 2 + 4). One could view the 16-bar unit as a phrase with two 8-bar subphrases or one could view it as two 8-bar phrases, each ending with a half cadence. Regardless of which of the two interpretations one chooses, the sentence model would still apply.

In-Class Activity 2.4

Diagram the phrase structure of mm. 1–16 in Mozart's Symphony No. 25, IV, and identify the phrase organization without the score. Listen to it twice. After the first hearing, identify the number of phrases. After the second, identify the cadence types and phrase structure.

Homework Assignment 2.3

Diagram the phrase structure of mm. 1–14 in Mozart's Symphony No. 40, III and then write a paragraph in which you compare that structure to a sentence. Could these phrases be thought of in terms of a 6-bar presentation and an 8-bar continuation? If one considers the first six bars to be composed of two phrases, does that make any comparison between this first section and a sentence unwarranted?

Homework Assignment 2.4

Choose a melody from the Baroque, Classical, or Romantic period that is not included in the Anthology and analyze its phrase organization by preparing an annotated score. To show its phrase organization, mark each phrase ending where it occurs with the cadence type below the system and each subphrase ending with a comma above the system. Then add brackets and all labels appropriate to the phrase organization above the systems (e.g. parallel period, antecedent, consequent). Your melody should be a minimum of 16 measures long.

Homework Assignment 2.5

Choose a tonal melody from the twentieth century that is not included in the Anthology and analyze its phrase organization by preparing an annotated score. To show its phrase organization, mark each phrase ending where it occurs with the cadence type below the system and each subphrase ending with a comma above the system. Then add brackets and labels appropriate to the phrase organization above the systems (e.g. parallel period, antecedent, consequent). Your melody should be a minimum of 16 measures long, and could be in any style (i.e. popular styles are fine).

Homework Assignment 2.6

Write a 1–2 page essay comparing phrase organization in the Baroque, Classical, and Romantic periods.

In More Detail: Periods within Sentences

Because periods and sentences are defined in very different ways, the two concepts do not have to be mutually exclusive. The first theme from Mozart's Symphony No. 40, I is an example of how one could find a period and a sentence within the same theme (for full score, see Anthology, pp. 315–316).

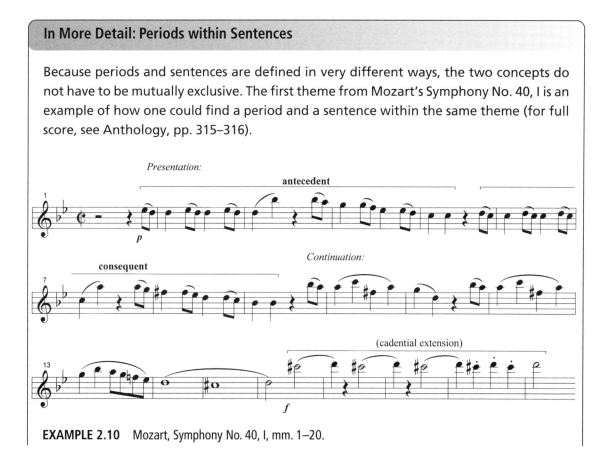

EXAMPLE 2.10   Mozart, Symphony No. 40, I, mm. 1–20.

One could view mm. 2–9 as a parallel period, but one could also view mm. 1–20 as a sentence because it shares the characteristic proportions and thematic relationships of the sentence: the basic idea is presented and then repeated (mm. 2–5 and 6–9), then the motive is developed (mm. 10–13), and that development is followed by a cadential gesture (mm. 14–17, extended to m. 20 through repetition). Thus, a period in the theme serves as the first half of a sentence.

Chapter Review

1   A **period** is a pair of phrases in which the second phrase ends with a more conclusive cadence than the first. Within the pair, the first phrase is called the **antecedent** and the second phrase is called the **consequent**.

2   A **phrase group** is a group of two or more phrases that seem to belong together, but don't form a period because the final cadence of the group is *not* more conclusive than the first.

3   In a **parallel period**, the second phrase begins with material from the first phrase, while in a **contrasting period**, the second phrase doesn't.

4   A **modulating period** is a period in which the second cadence is a more conclusive cadence type than the first, but is in a different key.

5   A **double period** is a group of four phrases presented as two pairs in which the second pair ends with a more conclusive cadence than the first pair. Note that, while the double period will be twice the length of a period, it *will not necessarily be made up of two periods*.

6   A **sentence** is a pair of phrases or subphrases that consists of a four-measure **presentation** followed by a four-measure **continuation**. In the presentation, a basic idea is presented and then repeated, with the repetition often varied to outline a different harmony. In the continuation, a motive from the basic idea is developed, and then that development is followed by a cadential gesture that brings the sentence to a close.

7   The primary difference between a period and a sentence is tied to how the two halves of each relate to one another. In a period, the consequent phrase sounds more like an independent unit and its cadence must be more conclusive than the one ending the antecedent phrase. In a sentence, the second half (continuation) sounds more like a development of material from the first half (presentation).

chapter 3

One-Part, Binary, and Ternary Forms

Many pieces or movements can be understood in terms of two or three sections, each of which is typically composed of multiple phrases that group together in various ways. There are many different ways that composers can articulate different sections—with literal repetition, new material, key changes, tempo changes, etc. This chapter primarily focuses on forms that can best be understood in terms of two or three sections.

One-Part Forms

One-part forms fall into two general categories: those that flow from beginning to end uninterrupted by any strong formal division (often because of a persistent rhythmic figuration pattern suggesting perpetual motion), and those that have an A A′ structure, in which the second half of the form is a varied repetition of the first. Preludes are often in one-part forms. Bach's Prelude in C Major from the *Well-Tempered Clavier*, Book I represents the first category of one-part forms mentioned above, while Chopin's Prelude in E Minor represents the second category. Listen to the two preludes while following the scores (see Anthology, pp. 4–5 and p. 219), paying special attention to the continuous structure of the Bach and the divided structure of the Chopin.

Binary Forms

Simple binary forms have two distinct sections, labeled A and B. They have the structure and repeat scheme shown in Formal Model 3.1 (see over). The Air from Bach's Orchestral Suite No. 3 is an example of a simple binary form; listen to it while following the score (see Anthology, pp. 14–15).

Simple binary forms usually have the following structure and repeat scheme (see over).

The B section often develops motivic material that was presented in the A section, but does not sound like a varied repetition of the A section, and the repeat scheme helps to clearly mark its beginning. The sectional repeats can be accomplished by actual repeat

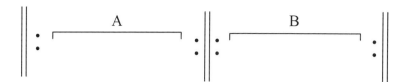

FORMAL MODEL 3.1   Simple Binary.

signs, or the repeats can be written out (i.e. "A A B B"). Note that upper-case letters are used to mark formal sections, and lower-case letters are used to mark phrases (as seen in Chapters 1 and 2).

The repeat scheme given in Formal Model 3.1 for simple binary is common in dance movements and sonata movements from the Baroque periods, and in minuets, trios, and scherzos from the Classical and Romantic periods as well. Lutheran chorales, such as the numerous chorales by J. S. Bach, are often in **bar form**, which can still be considered a kind of binary form, but with a different repeat scheme. In **bar form**, the first section is repeated, but the second section is not (i.e. "A A B"):

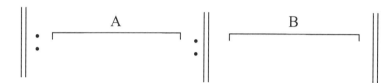

FORMAL MODEL 3.2   Bar Form (binary).

Bach's chorale setting of "Break Forth, Oh Beauteous Heavenly Light" is in this form; listen to it without the score.

The model for binary form shown in Formal Model 3.1 is called "simple binary," because there are two slightly more complex variations of it: *rounded binary* and *balanced binary*. **Rounded binary forms** have two distinct sections articulated by repeats like those found in simple binary forms, but in rounded binary forms, a modified (usually shortened) version of the A section returns after the B section.[1] The theme from the first movement of Mozart's K. 331 is an example of a rounded binary form; listen to it while following the score (see Anthology, p. 276).

Rounded binary forms usually have the following structure and repeat scheme:

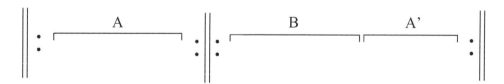

FORMAL MODEL 3.3   Rounded Binary.

---

[1] Some musicians use the term "incipient ternary" in place of what is called rounded binary here. This reflects the fact that, on first hearing, it sounds as though a true three-part (ternary) form is beginning to take shape (is *incipient*). The difference between rounded binary and ternary forms will be discussed after ternary forms are introduced.

The return of A (as A′) in a rounded binary sounds like a return to the beginning. It is not enough for just the thematic (melodic) material of the A section to return; an almost literal repetition of the opening material in all of the parts is needed, at least for a few measures, to signal a return of A and thus distinguish a rounded binary form.

Balanced binary forms have two distinct sections articulated by repeats like those found in simple binary forms, but in balanced binary forms, cadential material from the end of the A section returns at the end of the B section: The March from Bach's *Notebook for Anna Magdalena Bach* is an example of a balanced binary:

EXAMPLE 3.1 J. S. Bach, *Notebook for Anna Magdalena Bach*, "March."

Balanced binary forms usually have the following structure and repeat scheme:

$$\|:\quad \underset{(x)}{\underline{\qquad\qquad A \qquad\qquad}}\quad :\|:\quad \underset{(x)}{\underline{\qquad\qquad B \qquad\qquad}}\quad :\|$$

FORMAL MODEL 3.4   Balanced Binary.

Note: (x) = cadential material from the A section that returns to close the B section.

The return of the cadential material at the end of the B section may be transposed to a different key. Note that the word "balanced" as it is used here has nothing to do with how long the two sections are; the two sections could be of very different lengths and still create a balanced binary form. Rounded binary forms, in addition to having a return of the A section's opening material, often end with a return of the A section's cadential material. In such cases, they are still called rounded binary forms rather than balanced, because the return of cadential material in a balanced binary comes at the end of the *B section*; rounded binaries do not end with the B section at all—they end with a varied repetition of the A section.

The ending of the first section in any type of form is an important moment in the music, and there are two terms used to describe binary forms based on how the first section ends: *sectional* and *continuous*. A binary form is **sectional** if the first section ends with an authentic cadence in the home key; a binary form is **continuous** if the first section ends with a half cadence, or if it cadences in a secondary key. (One should note that some musicians use the terms "open" and "closed" in the way that "continuous" and "sectional" are defined here; "open" should be considered synonymous with "continuous," and "closed" should be considered synonymous with "sectional.") The theme from the first movement of Mozart's K. 331 (see Anthology, p. 276) is an example of a *sectional* rounded binary form, whereas the Air from Bach's Orchestral Suite No. 3 (see Anthology, pp. 14–15) is an example of a *continuous* simple binary form.

One critical aspect of understanding musical forms is knowing when and where to expect them. Movements from Baroque sonatas and dance suites are usually in some kind of continuous binary form. Minuets from the Classical and Romantic periods are also usually in binary form (though often sectional rather than continuous), as are scherzos (which replaced Minuets in the sonatas, symphonies, and string quartets of many Romantic composers).

In-Class Activity 3.1

Revisit the music covered in class and answer the following questions: What is the form of the Badinerie in J. S. Bach's Orchestral Suite No. 2 in B minor (see Anthology, pp. 13–14)? What is the form of the theme from Brahms' *Variations on a Theme by Haydn* (see Anthology, pp. 116–117)?

In-Class Activity 3.2

Identify cadences in the Badinerie from J. S. Bach's Orchestral Suite No. 2 in B minor *without the score* (it's in 2/4, but starts on beat 2). Then identify its form and diagram its phrase structure.

Homework Assignment 3.1

Listen to the Menuetto from Mozart's Symphony No. 40, III while following along with the score (see Anthology, pp. 333–334), and mark cadence points in the score as you listen. Then look at Homework Assignment 3.1 in your workbook, choose the incomplete phrase diagram that most closely matches the number of cadences you heard, fill in the blanks of that diagram with cadence types, measure numbers or key areas, as appropriate (blanks after arrows are for keys), and answer the question at the bottom of the page. Next, look at the incomplete phrase diagram that did not reflect your initial hearing, and fill in the blanks of that diagram. Finally, listen again while following this latter diagram and see if you can understand the logic behind the other interpretation.

Ternary Forms

Ternary forms have two distinct sections with a full return of the opening section at the end.

A   B   A

FORMAL MODEL 3.5   Ternary.

The B section of a ternary form is often in a contrasting key or group of keys. The return of the A section in a ternary form is an exact or almost exact repetition of the A section, not just a return of thematic content. Unlike the B sections of binary forms, which often develop material from the A section, the B sections of ternary forms usually present material that really sounds new.

There is an obvious similarity between rounded binary and ternary forms, and that similarity poses the following question: if one were to perform a rounded binary without the repeats, would the form then become ternary? Many would argue that such a question isn't fair, because it would be unmusical to ignore the repeats in a rounded binary. However, there are usually other differences between music in a ternary form and music in a rounded binary form: 1) often the return of A is abbreviated or altered in a rounded binary so that it almost feels like a coda to the first two sections; and 2) often the return of A in a rounded binary is set up at the end of the B section with a motion to the dominant, while that is not usually the case in a ternary form—the end of the B section in a ternary form seems more like a closing to something truly independent.

A *da capo aria*, one of the most common kinds of opera aria in the Baroque period, is ternary by definition; in a *da capo* aria, there is a first section ending with a double bar followed by a contrasting second section that ends with a double bar and the marking *da capo* ("the head"), which instructed the performers to return to the beginning and repeat the entire first section again. In *da capo* arias, it is also common to have an instrumental introduction in the A section that comes back to end that section, and may return in the middle of it as well (this is called a **ritornello**, a term that will be discussed more in Chapter 7). The aria "Non disperar" from Handel's opera *Giulio Cesare* is a good example; listen to it while following the score (see Anthology, pp. 220–221).

In operas from the Classical and Romantic periods, ternary forms were still often used in arias, even though other forms became common as well. However, in these later periods, composers would often write out a varied repetition of the first section rather than simply using a *da capo* marking.

In-Class Activity 3.3

Identify the form and diagram the phrase structure of the aria "L'empio, sleale, indegno" from Handel's *Giulio Cesare*, Act I, Scene 6 (see Anthology, pp. 222–224).

Homework Assignment 3.2

Listen to the aria "Non disperar" from Handel's *Giulio Cesare*, Act I, Scene 5 while following along with the score (see Anthology, pp. 220–221), and mark cadence points in the score as you listen (NB: note that the bass line of the score often changes to tenor clef). Then look at Homework Assignment 3.2 in your workbook. The incomplete phrase diagram given here may or may not reflect your interpretation. Fill in the blanks of that diagram with cadence types, sequence types, measure numbers or key areas, as appropriate, and answer the question at the bottom of the page, taking care to note the differences between your own interpretation and the one suggested in the workbook. Finally, listen again while following this diagram and see if you can understand the logic behind the interpretive choices that differed from your own.

In More Detail: Hemiolas as Cadential Devices in the Baroque Period

Notice that the cadences in mm. 12, 32, 44, 61, and 78 of the aria "L'empio, sleale, indegno" from Handel's *Giulio Cesare*, Act I, Scene 6 (see Anthology, pp. 222–224) are all preceded by a metrical feeling of three-against-two; this juxtaposition of metrical accents is called a **hemiola**. Hemiolas were commonly used at cadence points in the Baroque period when the music was in a fast triple meter. In each of the cited cadences above, the two 3/8 measures that precede the final chord of the cadence are grouped to suggest one larger measure of 3/4. A good practice/rehearsal technique for perfecting a hemiola is to practice conducting it while listening, and later, while singing one of the parts. Try conducting the aria with a one-beat conducting pattern from the beginning, but switch to a faster moving three-beat pattern to conduct each of the hemiolas (i.e. imagine that the quarter note is the beat in mm. 10–11, 30–31, 42–43, etc.).

Composite Forms

A **composite form** is one with component sections that can be broken down and understood in terms of formal models individually. For example, a ternary form with component sections that can each be understood as binary forms on their own is called a **composite ternary**. The third movement of a Classical or Romantic four-movement sonata, symphony, or string quartet is typically in a composite ternary form. These movements were often marked "Minuet and Trio" or "Scherzo and Trio," and in either case, it was common for composers to put a *da capo* at the end of the trio, so that the minuet or scherzo would be repeated in full to close the movement, thus creating a composite ternary. (One should note that some musicians use the term "compound ternary" in the way that "composite ternary" is defined here; therefore, "compound ternary" should be considered synonymous with "composite ternary.") In instrumental composite forms, the largest sections are usually in different (though often closely related) keys; this is one of the most effective ways that composers can group together the smaller sections into the larger ones.

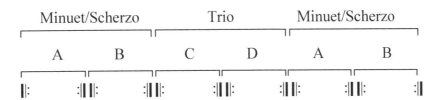

FORMAL MODEL 3.6 Minuet and Trio (composite ternary).

The third movement from Mozart's Symphony No. 40, III is a good example of a composite ternary; listen to it without the score and follow along using the model above.

While opera arias in the Baroque period were commonly *da capo* arias, and thus ternary by design, opera arias from the Classical period began to develop a composite binary form that led eventually to the standardized Italian Romantic opera aria shown in Formal Model 3.7. These arias begin with a recitative-like introduction that leads to a slow song in a binary or ternary form, then they segue into a free-form transitional passage that in turn leads to a *cabaletta*, a second song in a faster tempo that would typically also be in a binary or ternary form. Unlike in instrumental composite forms, in Italian Romantic opera arias, the two main parts of the aria were sometimes in the same key: the change in tempo and lyrics were enough to clearly distinguish the two.

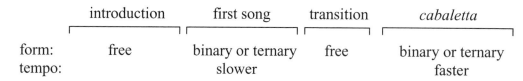

FORMAL MODEL 3.7 Italian Romantic Opera Aria (composite binary).

The aria "Ah fors'e lui . . . Sempre libera" from Verdi's *La Traviata* is a good example of a composite binary; listen to it without the score and follow along using the model (in this particular aria, the first song and the cabaletta are in two different keys).

Marches and Rags

Marches (such as those written by John Philip Sousa) and Rags (such as those written by Scott Joplin) are also typically **composite binary** forms. In a march, the two large sections that can be understood as binary forms by themselves are called the "March" and the "Trio", respectively, while the smaller sections are called "strains."

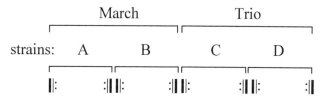

FORMAL MODEL 3.8 March (composite binary).

J. P. Sousa's "Stars and Stripes Forever" is one of the most famous marches in history; listen to it without the score and follow along using the model above.

In rags, the A strain comes back after the B strain to conclude the first section before the trio takes over, making a ternary form out of the first section.

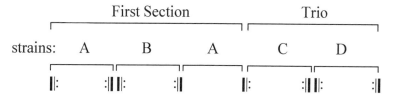

FORMAL MODEL 3.9 Rag (composite binary)

Scott Joplin's "Maple Leaf Rag" is one of the most famous rags in history; listen to it without the score and follow along using the model above.

In both marches and rags, the trio usually starts off in the key of the subdominant, which helps one to distinguish the two largest sections of the composite binary structure. In marches, it stays in that key all the way to the end, while in rags, the music will often return to the tonic key for the final strain.

> **In-Class Activity 3.4**
>
> Identify cadences in the Gavotte I from J. S. Bach's Orchestral Suite No. 3 in D major *without the score* (it's in 2/2, but starts on beat 2). Then identify its form and diagram its phrase structure.

Homework Assignment 3.3

Listen to the Gavotte II from J. S. Bach's Orchestral Suite No. 3 in D major twice, first while listening and conducting without the score and following the incomplete phrase diagram in Homework Assignment 3.3 of your workbook, and the second time while following along with the score (see Anthology, pp. 18–19), and marking cadence points in the score as you listen. Then fill in the blanks of the diagram with cadence types, sequence types, measure numbers or key areas, as appropriate, and answer the questions at the bottom of the page, taking care to note any differences between your own interpretation and the one suggested in the workbook. Finally, listen again while following this diagram and see if you can understand the logic behind the interpretive choices that differed from your own.

The 32-Bar Song Form

The **32-bar song form** (also sometimes called the *American Popular Ballad Form*) is a specific type of ternary form that emerged in the first half of the twentieth century with song composers such as George Gershwin, Cole Porter, Irving Berlin, Jerome Kern, and Richard Rodgers. The songs often began with a rubato introduction called a "verse" that would typically be through-composed (note that the meaning of the term "verse" in this context is different from its meaning in the context of today's popular music). The body of the song is called the "chorus" (again, a different use of a familiar term), and is in a ternary form where the music of the first A section is repeated, creating an AABA form, with each section typically being eight bars in length. While the music of the A section repeats twice, it sets new lines of text each time.

	A	A	B	A
mm.	1–8	9–16	17–24	25–32
lyrics:	*a*	*b*	*c*	*d*

FORMAL MODEL 3.10   32-Bar Song Form (ternary).

"Misty" by Erroll Garner and Johnny Burke is a good example of the American popular ballad form; listen to it without the score and follow along using the model above.

In-Class Activity 3.5

Identify the form and diagram the phrase structure of "You Took Advantage of Me," by Richard Rodgers and Lorenz Hart (as recorded by Carmen McRae). Do it without the score.

Form in Pop and Rock

Pop and rock songs from the 1950s until today often have very strongly defined musical forms, though there is great variety in which sections are repeated, how the sections are ordered, how long the sections are, etc. As mentioned before, the terms "verse" and "chorus" have different meanings when they are used to discuss pop and rock music than when they are used to discuss the 32-bar song form: in pop and rock, the "verse" is the part of the song that sets different lyrics each time it returns, whereas the "chorus" is the part of the song that returns with the same lyrics each time. What really defines "chorus" in the context of pop and rock is the return of both music and lyrics together (because of the repetition, the audience can—and often does—sing along with the performers during the chorus). Pop and rock songs can often be understood as some variation on the common form shown below:

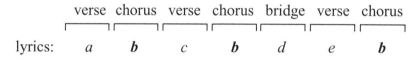

FORMAL MODEL 3.11   Common Form for a Pop and Rock Song.

"Please, Please Me" by the Beatles is a good example of the common form for a pop or rock song; listen to it and follow along using Formal Model 3.11.

In "Please, Please Me," the verse is just two four-bar phrases of music, and the chorus is just one long eight-bar phrase; together, the verse and chorus sound like a single section, and so the song could also be interpreted as a kind of AABA structure (where the A section = verse + chorus, and the B section = bridge). However, in the song "Satellite," by The Dave Matthews Band, there is a much stronger division between the verse and chorus (because of a change of meter from 3/4 to 6/8), and so the song form sounds more like it has three distinct sections (verse, chorus, bridge). Listen to "Satellite" and follow along using Formal Model 3.11.

Not all pop and rock songs have a bridge, but when there is one, it is generally a section that contrasts with the verse and chorus sharply enough to sound like its own section. If there is no bridge in a pop or rock song, there is sometimes an instrumental solo in its place, though instrumental solos could also be interjected at any point in the structure of a pop or rock song, whether there is a bridge or not. In "Revolution," by the Beatles, there is a very short instrumental solo in place of a bridge; listen to it and follow along using Formal Model 3.11.

Hearing Key Relationships

One way of making a new theme or section sound "new" is to put it in another key. Following key relationships without the score can be difficult, but the task is made much easier if one learns what to expect of different forms and historical periods. For example, Baroque sonatas in the major mode almost always modulate to the key of the dominant first, so if you are listening to the beginning of a sonata in D major by J. S. Bach, and then hear a modulation, you can count on this new key being A major. The tuning systems that were used in the Baroque and Classical periods in particular make the task of hearing modulations in the music easier, because they limited the choices available to those composers. Equal temperament was not established as a tuning system until the Romantic period, so composers usually limited themselves to **closely related keys**, keys that differ from the primary key by no more than one accidental. Of the closely related keys, the dominant and the relative major or minor are the most common secondary keys in tonal music. For any given primary key, there will be five other keys that are closely related to it.

EXAMPLE 3.2   Closely Related Keys to C Major and to G minor.

In-Class Activity 3.6

Identify the closely related keys to D major, placing them in a format like the one found in Example 3.2, and chart their use in the Air from Bach's Orchestral Suite No. 3 (see Anthology, pp. 14–15). Then identify the closely related keys to E major, placing them in a format like the one found in Example 3.2, and chart their use in the aria "Non disperar" from Handel's opera *Giulio Cesare* (see Anthology, pp. 220–221).

Perhaps because Baroque and Classical composers could not safely explore them without risking intonation problems, Romantic composers were drawn to **distantly related keys**, keys that differ from the primary key by more than one accidental. In particular, many Romantic composers had a fondness for **chromatic mediant relationships**—relationships between distantly related keys in which the two tonics are either a major third or a minor third apart. The exploration of distant key relationships in general, and of chromatic mediant relationships in particular, can be thought of as part of the sound of Romantic period music. There is a passage in the first movement of Brahms' Violin Concerto that illustrates chromatic mediant relations particularly well (see Anthology, pp. 211–212): a theme is first presented in F♯ major (mm. 445–457) before being transposed to the key of D major (mm. 458–461).

For any given primary key, there will be six other keys that are in a chromatic mediant relationship with it.[2]

F, Fm   F♯ (but not F♯m, because F♯m is closely related to D)

(D)

B♭, B♭m   B (but not Bm, because Bm is closely related to D)

EXAMPLE 3.3   Chromatic Mediants relative to D Major.

Chromatic mediant relationships are also important to film music, particularly to those with themes of science fiction or fantasy: the distant relationships they comprise can be thought of as mirroring the temporal and spatial distance between the world we live in and the world portrayed in the film (as George Lucas put it in the opening line to his science fiction epic *Star Wars*: "A long time ago, in a galaxy far, far away . . .").

In-Class Activity 3.7

Identify those keys in a chromatic mediant relationship with E♭ major, placing them in a format like the one in Example 3.17. Then do the same for E minor.

How to Identify Modulations When Listening Without the Score

1 Always be sure to orient yourself tonally by finding the tonic and singing through a tonic triad.
2 When you hear a modulation in a Baroque or Classical piece, you should expect that the new key is closely related to the primary key. If the mode of the new key is the same as the primary key, then you should first listen for the dominant. If the mode of the new key is different from the primary key, then you should first listen for the relative major/minor.
3 If the title of the piece leads you to expect a binary form (e.g. the movement is called "Gavotte" or "Minuet" or has the name of some other Baroque dance), then expect that any modulation in the first half will be to the dominant in a major-mode piece, and to the dominant or the relative major in a minor-mode piece (fairly easy to differentiate, since the key of the dominant in a minor-mode piece is minor, and the relative major is obviously major).
4 If the nature of a piece leads you to expect a ternary form (e.g. it's an opera aria or an art song), remember that the mediant, the submediant, or the subdominant are common choices for a secondary key, and use the mode to narrow down the choices even further (e.g. if the piece is in minor, and the B section is in major, then one should first listen for the mediant or submediant, since the subdominant would have been another minor key).

---

[2] Some authors define chromatic mediant relations as always being between keys that are of the same mode, and use the term "double chromatic mediants" to describe distant third relations between keys that are of different modes. See Stefan Kostka and Dorothy Payne, *Tonal Harmony with an Introduction to Twentieth-Century Music*, 6th ed (New York: McGraw-Hill, 2008).

Form in Vocal Music

The majority of forms found in vocal music are one-part, binary, or ternary forms, though one also finds variation forms, imitative forms, and rondo forms as well (see Chapters 5, 6, and 8). However, when composers set preexisting texts (as is common in art songs and Mass settings), the form and meaning of those texts sometimes lead them to musical forms not typically found in instrumental music. When studying any kind of vocal music, a careful consideration of the form and meaning of the text is essential to the understanding of its musical setting.

Strophic settings in vocal music are those that set different verses of a text to the same music. Church hymns are almost always strophic, as are many art songs. Schubert's "Heidenröslein" is a good example of a strophic art song; listen to it without the score. Note how all of the music—from beginning to end—is repeated three times, and each time the text set by the music changes.

Through-composed settings in vocal music are those that set each line of a text to new music, without any internal repetitions. Recitatives are almost always through-composed, as are some art songs. The recitative from Handel's *Giulio Cesare*, Act I, Scene 5 is a good example of this; listen to it without the score.

While the terms "strophic" and "through-composed" help to describe important aspects of musical form, they are not themselves forms, because they only describe the relationship between the text and its musical setting, not those relationships between the different parts or sections of the music that are independent of the text. For example, many of the chorales set by J. S. Bach are both strophic and in bar form. Listen to Bach's chorale setting of "Break Forth, Oh Beauteous Heavenly Light" again without the score; paying special attention to the strophic treatment of the A section.

A brief analysis of Schubert's "Kennst du das Land," D. 321, will illustrate how a song can be partially strophic and also how the meaning of the text can lead the composer to a form that is unlike any of the models discussed in this book. Example 3.4 shows how the stanzas fit within the repeat scheme, while Example 3.5 shows an English translation of the text by Goethe.

First, this song is a good example of a setting that is partially strophic: the first two sections are grouped together in a strophic setting of the first two stanzas, but the third stanza is set to new (albeit similar) music. Second, the song is a good example of how the meaning of the text sometimes leads a composer to a form that is unlike those commonly found in instrumental music. This form is *almost* a simple binary, but the repeat scheme

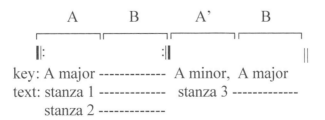

EXAMPLE 3.4 Repeat scheme of Schubert's "Kennst du das Land," D. 321.

Kennst du das Land, wo die Zitronen blühn,	Knowest thou where the lemon blossom grows,
Im dunkeln Laub die Gold-Orangen glühn,	In foliage dark the orange golden glows,
Ein sanfter Wind vom blauen Himmel weht,	A gentle breeze blows from the azure sky,
Die Myrte still und hoch der Lorbeer steht?	Still stands the myrtle, and the laurel, high?
Kennst du es wohl?	Dost know it well?
Dahin! dahin	'Tis there! 'Tis there
Möcht ich mit dir, o mein Geliebter, ziehn.	Would I with thee, oh my beloved, fare.
Kennst du das Haus? Auf Säulen ruht sein Dach.	Knowest the house, its roof on columns fine?
Es glänzt der Saal, es schimmert das Gemach,	Its hall glows brightly and its chambers shine,
Und Marmorbilder stehn und sehn mich an:	And marble figures stand and gaze at me:
Was hat man dir, du armes Kind, getan?	What have they done, oh wretched child, to thee?
Kennst du es wohl?	Dost know it well?
Dahin! dahin	'Tis there! 'Tis there
Möcht ich mit dir, o mein Beschützer, ziehn.	Would I with thee, oh my protector, fare.
Kennst du den Berg und seinen Wolkensteg?	Knowest the mountain with the misty shrouds?
Das Maultier sucht im Nebel seinen Weg;	The mule is seeking passage through the clouds;
In Höhlen wohnt der Drachen alte Brut;	In caverns dwells the dragons' ancient brood;
Es stürzt der Fels und über ihn die Flut!	The cliff rocks plunge under the rushing flood!
Kennst du ihn wohl?	Dost know it well?
Dahin! dahin	'Tis there! 'Tis there
Geht unser Weg! O Vater, laß uns ziehn!	Leads our path! Oh father, let us fare.
poetry by J. W. Goethe, 1799	English translation by Walter Meyer

EXAMPLE 3.5   Schubert's "Kennst du das Land," D. 321, English translation.

associated with binary is missing, and Schubert also varies the material of the A section when he sets the third stanza. Schubert's desire to paint the beginning of the third stanza in a darker color than the first two leads him to shift the mode of the A section to minor and to change the dynamic to *forte* at that point, creating an A′ (he makes some other structural changes as well). The mood at the beginning of the first two stanzas is happy—"the lemon blossom grows," "a gentle breeze blows from the azure sky," "[the house's] hall glows brightly and its chambers shine"—but the mood in the third stanza is strikingly different— "in caverns dwells the dragons' ancient brood; The cliff rocks plunge under the rushing flood!"—and so on. Schubert's choice to alter the A section so that it better fits the change in the text reflects a sensitivity to the texts in vocal music shared by most great composers throughout history. This analysis should underscore that one cannot truly understand musical forms in vocal works without first understanding the form and meaning of their texts.

Homework Assignment 3.4

Look at Homework Assignment 3.4 in your workbook, and listen to the third movement from Mozart's *Eine kleine Nachtmusik* without the score while conducting along in 3/4. Use the steady meter and the repeat scheme to follow along with the diagram. Then fill in the blanks of the diagram with cadence types, measure numbers or key areas, as appropriate, and answer the questions at the bottom of the page, taking care to note any differences between your own interpretation and the one suggested by the diagram. Finally, listen again while following the diagram and see if you can understand the logic behind the interpretive choices that differed from your own.

Homework Assignment 3.5

Look at Homework Assignment 3.5 in your workbook, and listen to Josephine Lang's "Oh ich manchmal dein Gedanke" without the score while conducting along in 3/4. Use the steady meter to follow along with the diagram. Then fill in the blanks of the diagram with cadence types, measure numbers or key areas, as appropriate, and follow the instructions in the paragraph that follows it. Finally, listen again while following the diagram and see if you can understand the logic behind any interpretive choices that differed from your own.

Homework Assignment 3.6

Look at Homework Assignment 3.6 in your workbook, and listen to the first twenty-three measures of the Courante from Elisabeth Jacquet de la Guerre's *Pièces de clavecin* while following along with the score, marking cadence points in the score as you listen. Then choose the incomplete phrase diagram that most closely matches the number of cadences you heard, and fill in the blanks of that diagram with cadence types, sequence types, measure numbers or key areas, as appropriate (blanks after arrows are for keys). Next, look at the incomplete phrase diagram that did not reflect your initial hearing, fill in the blanks of that diagram, and answer the questions at the bottom of the page. Finally, listen again while following this latter diagram and see if you can understand the logic behind the other interpretation.

Homework Assignment 3.7

Choose a binary or ternary art song from the Baroque, Classical, or Romantic period that is not included in the Anthology. Analyze its form, phrase structure, key areas, and harmonic sequences by preparing an annotated score. Label the sections on the score where each new section begins, and if it is binary, label the specific type of binary at the beginning of the score. To show its phrase structure, mark each phrase ending where it occurs with the cadence type below the system and each subphrase ending with a comma above the system. Also, label key areas and harmonic sequences (by type) where they occur.

Homework Assignment 3.8

Choose a binary or ternary movement from a Baroque, Classical, or Romantic-period choral work or instrumental chamber work that is not included in the Anthology. Analyze its form, phrase structure, key areas, and harmonic sequences by preparing an annotated score. Label the sections on the score where each new section begins, and if it is binary, label the specific type of binary at the beginning of the score. To show its phrase structure, mark each phrase ending where it occurs with the cadence type below the system and each subphrase ending with a comma above the system. Also, label key areas and harmonic sequences (by type) where they occur.

Homework Assignment 3.9

Write a 1–2 page essay comparing rounded binary form with ternary form.

Chapter Review

1   A **simple binary form** has two distinct sections, labeled A and B, and each section is repeated.

2   A **rounded binary form** has two distinct sections articulated by repeats like those found in a simple binary form, but in rounded binary forms, a modified (usually shortened) version of the A section returns after the B section. The return of A almost feels like a coda to the first two sections, and is usually set up at the end of the B section with a motion to the dominant.

3   A **balanced binary form** has two distinct sections articulated by repeats like those found in a simple binary form, but in balanced binary forms, cadential material from the end of the A section returns at the end of the B section.

4   The B section of a binary form often develops motivic material that was presented in the A section, but does not sound like a varied repetition of the A section, and the repeat scheme helps to clearly mark its beginning. The sectional repeats can be accomplished by actual repeat signs, or the repeats can be written out (i.e. "A A B B"). Note that upper-case letters are used to mark formal sections, while lower-case letters are used to mark phrases (as seen in Chapters 1 and 2).

5   A binary form is **sectional** if the first section ends with an authentic cadence in the home key; a binary form is **continuous** if the first section ends with a half cadence, or if it cadences in a secondary key.

6   Movements from Baroque sonatas and dance suites are usually in some kind of continuous binary form. Minuets, Trios, and Scherzos from the Classical and Romantic periods are often in some kind of binary form, though they are often sectional rather than continuous. Lutheran chorales (like those by Bach) are usually in **bar form**, which is a binary form with the repeat scheme AAB instead of the AABB scheme found in simple, rounded, and balanced binary.

7   A **ternary form** has two distinct sections with a full return of the opening section at the end. The B section of a ternary form is often in a contrasting key or group of

keys. Unlike the B sections of binary forms, the B sections of ternary forms usually present material that really sounds new.

8 A **composite form** is one with A and B sections that can be broken down into smaller sections and understood in terms of formal models individually (usually binary forms). The third movement of a Classical or Romantic four-movement sonata, symphony, or string quartet (when marked "Minuet and Trio" or "Scherzo and Trio") is typically in a composite ternary form. Marches and rags are typically in composite binary forms.

9 A *da capo aria*, one of the most common kinds of opera aria in the Baroque period, is in a ternary form. In operas from the Classical and Romantic periods, ternary forms were still often used in arias; however, in these later periods, composers often wrote out a varied repetition of the first section rather than simply using a *da capo* marking. In the Romantic period, a specific kind of composite binary aria became standard in Italian opera. These arias begin with a recitative-like introduction that leads to a slow song in a binary or ternary form, then they segue into a free-form transitional passage that in turn leads to a *cabaletta*, a second song in a faster tempo that would typically also be in a binary or ternary form.

10 The **32-bar song form** is a ternary form where the music of the first A section is repeated, creating an AABA form, with each section typically being eight bars long. While the music of the A section repeats twice, it sets new lines of text each time. In 32-bar song forms, the body of the form is called the **chorus**, while the rubato introduction is called the **verse**.

11 In pop and rock songs, the **verse** is the part of the song that sets different lyrics each time it returns, whereas the **chorus** is the part of the song that returns with the same lyrics each time. What really defines "chorus" in the context of pop and rock is the return of both music and lyrics together (because of the repetition, the audience can—and often does—sing along with the performers during the chorus). Pop and rock songs can often be understood as some variation of the following form: verse, chorus, verse, chorus, bridge, verse, chorus.

12 Keys that differ from the primary key by no more than one accidental are called **closely related keys**; keys that differ from the primary key by more than one accidental are called **distantly related keys. Chromatic mediants** are distantly related keys with tonics that are either a major third or a minor third apart.

13 **Strophic** settings in vocal music are those that set different verses of a text to the same music (like church hymns). **Through-composed** settings in vocal music are those that set each line of a text to new music, without any internal repetitions (like recitatives).

14 When studying any kind of vocal music, a careful consideration of the form and meaning of the text is essential to the understanding of its musical setting.

chapter 4

Sonata Forms

One of the most important developments in instrumental music of the Classical period was the development of sonata form. As will be shown, sonata form has elements in common with both rounded binary and ternary forms, but is more detailed and complicated as a model than either one. This chapter will focus on sonata form, and in subsequent chapters we will see two other important variants of sonata form: Classical concerto form (Chapter 7) and sonata-rondo form (Chapter 8).

The Three Parts of Sonata Forms

A **sonata form** has three large sections: the *exposition*, the *development*, and the *recapitulation*. The **exposition** is the first section, in which the most important themes of the movement are presented. The **development** is the second section, in which the themes from the exposition are developed. The **recapitulation** is the last section, and is a varied repetition of the exposition. Sonata form has two sets of repeats, with the end of the first set and the beginning of the second occurring between the exposition and the development. In this way, as well as many others, it can be thought of as a more complex version of rounded binary (below).

However, there are also compelling reasons for understanding sonata form as a more complex version of ternary. One is that movements in sonata form are typically much longer than movements in rounded binary form, and proportions affect the way we hear musical forms. While many would argue that it is unmusical to ignore the repeats in a rounded binary, just as many would argue that it's justifiable in some sonata form movements simply because the sheer length of a performance with the repeats taken would be taxing on any audience (for example, consider the first movement of Beethoven's *Eroica* Symphony, a sonata form that is 691 measures long without taking the repeat of the exposition!). Since its repeat scheme is one important reason that a rounded binary movement *sounds* binary, the question of repeats is very important to how one interprets the largest structure of sonata form. Also, the second set of repeats in the model for sonata

Rounded Binary

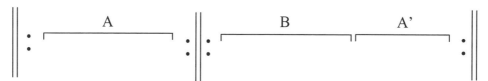

Largest Sections of Sonata Form

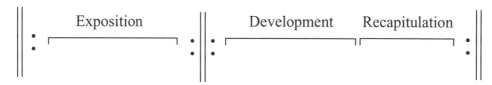

FORMAL MODEL 4.1   Rounded Binary Compared to Sonata Form.

form given above were typically not present in Romantic period sonata forms, only in those from the Classical period.

Another important argument for a ternary interpretation of sonata form is that the recapitulation in a sonata form is usually at least as long if not longer than the exposition. It is more common in a rounded binary form for the last section to be roughly half the length of the beginning section.

Tonal Structure and Thematic Organization

Though the question of binary versus ternary in understanding sonata form is still debated by musicians, those on both sides of the debate would agree that it really deserves to be understood as a form in its own right, regardless of the elements it has in common with rounded binary or ternary. There is one important element that makes sonata form unique: a large-scale tonal tension between the primary key and a secondary key (its dominant or relative major) is created in the exposition, a tension that is heightened in the development through tonal instability before it eventually resolves in the recapitulation.

The arrival of the new secondary key in the exposition is always accompanied by the presentation of important thematic material. Usually this material is a secondary theme,

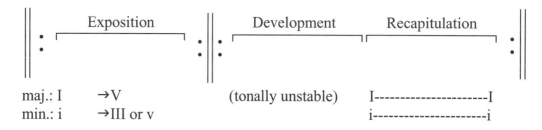

(Roman numerals indicate key areas)

FORMAL MODEL 4.2   Key Relations in Sonata Form.

but in the Classical period it was sometimes just a transposition of the first theme (such sonata forms are called *monothematic*; e.g. Haydn, Piano Sonata, Hob. XVI/36, I).

The Exposition

Expositions in sonata forms can be understood as having four parts, presented in the following order: a *primary theme*, a *bridge*, a *secondary theme*, and a *closing*. The first part is defined by the presentation of a theme or themes: a primary theme or group of themes is presented in the key of the tonic (in the Classical period, only one primary theme was typically used, but over the course of the Romantic period more composers began to substitute a group of themes in this first part). The second part, the bridge, is so named because it bridges a gap between one key and another, modulating to the new key with material that is not as thematically important (often with sequences, scalar runs, motivic repetitions, and cadential gestures).[1] The third part is defined by the presentation of a secondary theme (or theme group) in a secondary key. The fourth part, the closing, is so named because it serves to bring the exposition to a close (often with sequences, scalar runs, motivic repetitions, and cadential gestures), and confirms the secondary key of the exposition.

In major-mode sonata forms, the secondary theme (or theme group) is in the key of the dominant; in minor-mode sonata forms, it is either in the key of the dominant or in the key of the relative major (e.g. in a C-minor sonata form, the secondary theme would be in either E♭ major or G minor). Example 4.1 shows a diagram of the parts of the exposition in the first movement to Mozart's Symphony No. 40 in G minor:

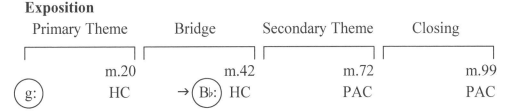

EXAMPLE 4.1   Diagram of Exposition in Mozart's Symphony No. 40, I.

Compare this diagram to the music (see Anthology, pp. 315–320). Note that the end of the exposition in m. 99 is easy to find because of the repeat sign in m. 100 (the end of the exposition is taken to be m. 99 because of the cadence ending in that measure; m. 100 serves as a kind of anacrusis to m. 1 and, on the second time through, to the first measure of the development section.)

In an exposition, one part often flows seamlessly into the next, and so it is often hard to tell where one part ends and the next begins. Some musicians might feel that the end of the primary theme is actually in m. 28, and is elided with the beginning of the bridge in that measure. Such an interpretation is no better or worse than the one given above. The

---

[1] One should note that what is called the "bridge" here is called the "transition" by some musicians. In the context of sonata form expositions, one should read the terms "bridge" and "transition" as synonyms.

difficulty in discerning the beginnings and endings of the parts in an exposition is a typical feature of sonata form, and is one reason they are called "parts" of the exposition here, rather than "sections": the term "section" implies a more definitive beginning and ending than one often gets within the exposition.

In-Class Activity 4.1

Diagram the phrase structure of the exposition to Mozart's Symphony No. 40, I, and be sure to label any forms of phrase organization by type (e.g. periods, sentences, etc.).

The Development

Development sections are so named because they primarily develop material from the exposition, though occasionally one finds a genuinely new theme there. The primary methods for developing materials in a development section are motivic repetition (often varied repetition) and sequences (both melodic and harmonic). Often development sections are tonally unstable, with frequent modulations; the passages in keys most distantly related to the primary key are generally found there. Development sections often end on a dominant pedal in the primary key. Example 4.2 diagrams the phrase structure of the development section in Mozart's Symphony No. 40 in G minor, I.

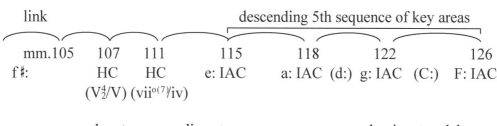

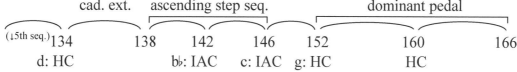

EXAMPLE 4.2   Phrase Diagram of Development in Mozart's Symphony No. 40, I.

Compare this diagram to the music (see Anthology, pp. 320–324). This development section is a good example of what one expects to find. The primary theme is developed throughout, though it never appears in its entirety: at the beginning, just the first phrase is developed, and by the end, it is just the head motive (i.e. the first motive of the first theme) that remains. The tonal instability is heard immediately, as the first phrase of the primary theme begins in F♯ minor, and then is harmonized with a descending chromatic bass line that carries the music to E minor. Note that both of these keys are distantly related to the primary key of the movement, G minor (the key signatures of G minor and F♯ minor differ by five accidentals, while those of G minor and E minor differ by three accidentals). Development sections are the one place that Classical composers would explore distantly related keys—elsewhere they almost always adhered to closely related keys.

Beginning in m. 115 and continuing until m. 126, a descending fifth sequence of key areas (not of chord roots) drives the music through the following keys: E minor, A minor, D minor, G minor, C major, and F major. At that point a harmonic descending fifth sequence takes over (chord roots: F–B♭–E♭–A–D) and drives straight through B♭ major to a half cadence in D minor, which is extended to last five measures (mm. 134–138). During that cadential extension, the melodic material is shortened to just the first nine notes of the primary theme.

What follows in mm. 138–145 is a harmonic ascending step sequence (chord roots: F-B♭–G–C) that takes the music from B♭ minor to C minor. This leads finally to a phrase ending with a half cadence in G minor, immediately after which the dominant pedal on D begins in m. 152, accompanied by a further shortening of the melodic material to just the first three notes. The dominant pedal lasts right up until the beginning of the recapitulation in m. 165 (note that the melodic return of the first theme is actually in m. 164, a full bar earlier than the return of its accompaniment from the exposition).

In summary, this development section meets expectations in the following ways: 1) it develops a theme from the exposition by shortening it into smaller and smaller units and transposing those units to a variety of other keys; 2) it is tonally unstable, because it modulates often, and explores keys that are distantly related to the primary key; 3) it relies heavily on sequences; and 4) it ends on a dominant pedal.

The Recapitulation

The recapitulation is a varied repetition of the exposition, and thus can also be understood as having the same four parts, presented in the same order: *primary theme* (or *theme group*), *bridge, secondary theme* (or *theme group*), *closing*. The main difference between the recapitulation and the exposition is that in the recapitulation, the secondary theme is transposed to the primary key, thus resolving the tonal tension between primary and secondary key areas that is found in the exposition. Because the bridge in the exposition modulates to the secondary key, that section is often substantially rewritten in the recapitulation. Example 4.3 diagrams the parts of the recapitulation in the first movement of Mozart's Symphony No. 40 in G minor.

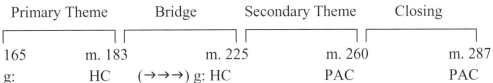

EXAMPLE 4.3 Diagram of Recapitulation in Mozart's Symphony No. 40, I.

Note that while the bridge in the exposition was only twenty-two measures long, the bridge in the recapitulation is forty-two measures long. Compare the two bridges: mm. 21–42 and mm. 183–224. While the bridge in the exposition moves directly from G minor to the relative major without going through any other keys, the bridge in the recapitulation goes through E♭ major and F minor, and then into a descending fifths sequence in C minor (mm. 202–207) before settling back into the key of G minor. The two bridges are different because they have different goals: the one in the exposition is aiming for B♭ major, while the one in the recapitulation is aiming to end back in the tonic key.

In-Class Activity 4.2

Diagram the phrase structure of the recapitulation to Mozart's Symphony No. 40, I, and be sure to label any forms of phrase organization by type (e.g. periods, sentences, etc.).

Homework Assignment 4.1

Listen to the first movement from Haydn's Sonata in C minor, Hob. XVI: 20 while following along with the score (see Anthology, pp. 234–239), and mark cadence points in the score as you listen. Then look at the incomplete phrase diagram given in Homework Assignment 4.1 of your workbook; this diagram may or may not reflect your interpretation. Fill in the blanks with formal labels (e.g. exposition, primary theme, bridge, etc.), cadence types, sequence types, measure numbers or key areas, as appropriate (blanks before colons are for keys), and answer the question at the bottom of the page, taking care to note the differences between your own interpretation and the one suggested in the workbook. Finally, listen again while following this diagram and see if you can understand the logic behind the interpretive choices that differed from your own. Note that there is no bridge in the recapitulation!

Introductions and Codas

Introductions and codas are never considered to be part of the standard musical forms, but are always options for the composer; movements in sonata form can be preceded by an introduction before the sonata form itself begins, and can conclude with a coda that begins after the sonata form itself is over. When a sonata-form movement includes an introduction, the introduction is almost always markedly slower than the sonata form itself (e.g. Haydn's Symphony No. 103 begins *Adagio*, then the exposition arrives *Allegro con Spirito* in m. 40); the dramatic tempo change helps to mark the beginning of the exposition for the listener. In Mozart's Symphony No. 40, a short coda is elided to the end of the recapitulation and helps to bring the music to a close (see mm. 285–end).

Sonata Form in Review

One should memorize the key elements of sonata form as follows:

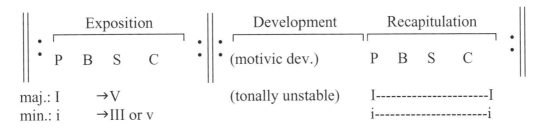

P = Primary Theme, B = Bridge, S = Secondary Theme, C = Closing
(Roman numerals indicate key areas)

FORMAL MODEL 4.3   Sonata Form.

As a review of this basic model and how it is realized in actual works, study the first movement of Beethoven's Symphony No. 5 and compare the score to the following diagrams as you listen to it (see Anthology, pp. 97–112).

In the recapitulation, note that the second theme is transposed to the level of the primary tonic but that the mode of the key is major, not minor. The conflict between the competing tonics C and E♭ that was established in the exposition is still resolved to a

Exposition

Primary Theme	Bridge	Secondary Theme	Closing
m.33	m.58	m.94	m.122
c: IAC	→ E♭: HC	HC	PAC

EXAMPLE 4.4   Diagram of Exposition in Beethoven's Symphony No. 5, I.

link	a1	b1	b2	b3	b4	b5	c1
128	137	145	153	158	164	179	187
f: HC	HC	→c: HC	→g: HC	IAC	IAC	HC	IAC

c2	c3	d1	link	link
195	215	228	249	252
→c: IAC	→f♯: IAC	prog.cad.	→c: IAC	HC

EXAMPLE 4.5   Development in Beethoven's Symphony No. 5, I.

Note: Phrases labeled "a" above develop material from the first half of the primary theme, phrases labeled "b" develop material from the second half of the primary theme, and phrases labeled "c" develop material from the second theme.

Recapitulation

Primary Theme	Bridge	Secondary Theme	Closing	(Coda)
m. 277	m. 302	m. 346	m. 374	
c: IAC	HC; C:	PAC	PAC	

EXAMPLE 4.6 Diagram of Recapitulation in Beethoven's Symphony No. 5, I.

unifying C, but the second theme retains more of its original character by keeping the same mode it had in the exposition (compare the treatment of the second theme here to the treatment of the second theme in the first movement of Mozart's Symphony No. 40, where both the tonic and the mode of the second theme change in the recapitulation).

In-Class Activity 4.3

Identify the formal sections in Beethoven's Piano Sonata No. 1, I and discuss its phrase structure (see Anthology, pp. 34–37).

In-Class Activity 4.4

Identify the formal sections in Beethoven's Symphony No. 3, I (see Anthology, pp. 64–96).

Homework Assignment 4.2

Listen to the development section from the first movement of Beethoven's Symphony No. 3 while following along with the score (see Anthology, pp. 71–83), and mark cadence points in the score as you listen. Then look at the incomplete phrase diagram given in Homework Assignment 4.2 of your workbook; this diagram may or may not reflect your interpretation. Fill in the blanks with cadence types, sequence types, measure numbers or key areas, as appropriate (blanks after arrows are for keys), and answer the question at the end.

In More Detail: The Origins of Sonata Form

Historians have argued for various genres when attempting to identify the antecedents to sonata form. Many point to the similarities between rounded binary and sonata form: the second half is generally longer than the first, the repeat scheme is the same, the material immediately after the first set of repeats is usually developmental, and most importantly there is a return to the initial thematic material. Others point to the concertos, overtures, and arias of the Baroque, because the thematic contrast one often finds in those genres is similar to the kind of thematic contrast one often finds between first and second themes in a sonata form.

Though one can see clear examples of sonata form as early as the 1730s, one should note that sonata form as it is described in this chapter did not immediately replace binary form in the instrumental music of composers from that time; it was a gradual transition that gained momentum with the popularity of Haydn's music, but one can still find binary form in the first movements of sonatas well into the 1750s (e.g. in Domenico Scarlatti's keyboard sonatas).

The Four-Movement Model

As was mentioned in the preceding chapter, one critical aspect of understanding musical forms is knowing when and where to expect them. One should memorize the standard model for four-movement sonatas, symphonies, and string quartets in the Classical and Romantic periods.

I.   Fast; Sonata Form; Primary Key
II.   Slow; variable (Sonata Form and Theme and Variations are common); Contrasting Key
III. Classical period: Medium triple meter; Minuet and Trio (composite ternary); Primary Key.
      Romantic period: Fast triple meter; Scherzo and Trio (composite ternary); Primary Key or Contrasting Key
IV.   Fast; Rondo (to be discussed in Chapter 8), Sonata-Rondo (also to be discussed in Chapter 8), or Sonata Form; Primary Key

FORMAL MODEL 4.4   Classical and Romantic Four-Movement Model.

One deviation from the four-movement model can be found in the Romantic period easily enough that it deserves special mention: sometimes the second and third movements sound like these models are reversed: the second movement is a fast scherzo and trio, while the third movement is the slowest movement (e.g. Beethoven's Ninth Symphony).

There are a great number of sonatas, symphonies, and string quartets that have less than, or more than, four movements, as well as many that have four movements, but do not follow the above model. (Deviations from this model are much more frequent in the Romantic period than in the Classical.) This model, just like all of the models in this book, should be understood as a generalization, not as some kind of tool for assessing artistic worth. Nevertheless, such models are useful in understanding the expectations of musicians and audience members, and can also help the music student who is trying to absorb the most famous pieces of tonal music, since they can serve to aid in memory. For example, the second movement to Beethoven's Ninth Symphony is a Scherzo; this actually makes it stand out among his second movements, because none of the others are.

In-Class Activity 4.5

Identify the formal sections in Haydn's Symphony No. 103, I (see Anthology, pp. 258–275).

Homework Assignment 4.3

Listen to the first movement from Haydn, Symphony No. 103 while following along with the score (see Anthology, pp. 258–275), and mark cadence points in the score as you listen. Then look at the incomplete phrase diagram given in Homework Assignment 4.3 of your workbook; this diagram may or may not reflect your interpretation. Fill in the blanks with formal labels (e.g. exposition, primary theme, bridge, etc.), cadence types, sequence types, measure numbers or key areas, as appropriate.

Sonata Form in Fast Movements and Slow Movements

Sonata form was used in fast-paced first movements so often during the Classical and Romantic periods that there is a tradition of calling the form "Sonata Allegro," a tradition that persists to this day. However, it is important to note that sonata form was sometimes also used in slow-paced second movements, though many other forms were used as well (e.g. the slow movements in both Beethoven's First and Second Symphonies are in sonata form). Some generalizations about the character of the form as it is found in a fast tempo do not apply when looking at the form in a slow tempo. In first-movement sonata forms, the primary theme is typically bold and powerful, while the second theme is more lyrical; in second-movement sonata forms this generalization is no longer useful. Other common differences between first and second movement sonata forms include the use of repeats (less common in second movements), and dramatic changes in dynamics and texture (again, less common in second movements). When listening without the score, one can still use several audible markers to keep track of the different sections of sonata form as a movement unfolds.

How to Identify the Parts of a Sonata Form When Listening Without the Score

1 If one hears an opening slow section, followed by a fast section, this is the slow introduction followed by the beginning of the exposition. The first thematic material one hears in the fast section is the first theme of the sonata form. However, remember that not all sonata forms begin with an introduction, and one should not expect to find an introduction to a sonata form in a second movement.

2 The bridge is marked by its modulation. It is sometimes hard to tell exactly where the bridge starts, but when one hears the key changing for the first time, one is usually hearing the bridge of the exposition.

3 The second theme is often set up by a large cadence on the dominant of either the home key or the secondary key (the key of the dominant or of the relative major) at the end of the bridge, and often this is accompanied by a large rhythmic and textural break (in first-movement sonata forms, the second theme is softer and more lyrical).

4   The closing section can often be identified by melodic material that seems less thematic and by a shift to thicker scoring and louder dynamics. The closing section is also very emphatic in stating the key, and often features strongly cadential progressions. Like the move from first theme to bridge, it is sometimes hard to tell exactly where the second theme ends and the closing section starts.

5   The development is easy to identify if the traditional repeat of the exposition is observed, because the first new material after all that repetition should stand out. However, in addition to just listening for the end of repeated material, one also commonly finds a dramatic thinning of the texture and softer dynamics. Another common cue that the development has started in major-mode sonata forms is a shift to the minor mode; because both the primary key and the secondary key in the exposition will be major for a major-mode sonata, the shift is very noticeable.

6   The development often ends with a pedal on the dominant, and the recapitulation almost always begins with the first theme, usually presented in a manner than recalls the opening of the exposition.

7   The recapitulation is a varied repetition of the exposition, but the amount of variation can be great or small, depending upon the composer. The main differences one can hear are the change to the bridge (in the exposition, it is responsible for modulating to a secondary key, but its harmonic goal changes in the recapitulation to become the primary key), and the change to the second theme (formerly in the secondary key, now in the primary key).

8   If a coda is to be included, the closing material from the exposition is often changed quite a bit in the recapitulation to better lead into the coda. In the Romantic period, some codas started to take on characteristics that are typically associated with the development section. Thus, if motivic development or what sounds like new material follows the closing material, one is probably hearing a coda.

In More Detail: Deviations from the Sonata Form Model

Almost every conceivable variant on the basic structure of sonata form was explored in the nineteenth century. To explore the full range of possibilities would be beyond the scope of this book; some sonata forms have expositions in which three keys are established as important (e.g. Brahms, Symphony No. 2, I), some have recapitulations that start in a key other than the primary key (e.g. Mozart, Piano Sonata, K. 545, I), some have recapitulations in which the second theme comes before the first (e.g. Beethoven, String Quartet, Op. 59/3, I), and so on. It is important to realize that such departures from the model for sonata form neither discredit this model nor discredit the work that varies from the model as somehow ill-formed. The model is an abstraction based on what happened most often in Classical-period sonatas, symphonies, and string quartets and in the works of composers influenced by Haydn, Mozart, and Beethoven (this would describe most if not all Romantic composers, and a great number of twentieth-century composers as well). It is a great backdrop against which to understand the form of a wide range of musical works, but is not meant to be used as a standard of judgment. To interpret a deviation from the sonata form model as a sign of incompetence on the part of the composer would be foolish. Great composers are generally experts at musical forms, and it is precisely that understanding that gives them the confidence to make changes to a model that has proven to be a valuable resource for those that preceded them.

Sonata Forms Without Development Sections

In the second movements of Classical and Romantic period sonatas, symphonies and string quartets, one will sometimes find a sonata form which has an exposition and a recapitulation, but does not have a development section; in place of a development section, there is just a brief transition that links the exposition to the recapitulation (e.g. Beethoven, Piano Sonata, Op. 10, No. 1, II). Sonata forms without development sections are also commonly found in Classical period overtures (e.g. Mozart's *Marriage of Figaro* Overture). Sonata forms without developments sections are sometimes called *sonatina forms*, which can be confusing, since the difference between sonatas and sonatinas as instrumental genres really relates to the length and seriousness of the works, not their forms. It is not uncommon to find a sonata form as the first movement of a sonatina (e.g. Kuhlau, Sonatina, Op. 20, No. 1, I), and one will often find a sonata form without a development section in the slow second movement of a four-movement work from the Classical and Romantic period.

Homework Assignment 4.4

Listen to the first movement from Mozart's *Eine kleine Nachtmusik* while following along with the score (see Anthology, pp. 288–291), and mark cadence points in the score as you listen. Then look at the incomplete phrase diagram given in Homework Assignment 4.4 of your workbook; this incomplete phrase diagram may or may not reflect your interpretation. Fill in the blanks with formal labels (e.g. exposition, primary theme, bridge, etc.), cadence types, sequence types, measure numbers or key areas.

Homework Assignment 4.5

Listen to the first movement of Beethoven's Piano Sonata, Op. 13 and mark its phrase structure directly on the score (this is not included in the Anthology). Then look at the incomplete phrase diagram given in Homework Assignment 4.5 of your workbook; this diagram may or may not reflect your interpretation. Fill in the blanks with formal labels (e.g. exposition, primary theme, bridge, etc.), cadence types, measure numbers or key areas, as appropriate. Then answer the questions that follow the diagram.

Homework Assignment 4.6

Listen to the first movement of Fanny Mendelssohn-Hensel's Trio in D minor, Op. 11 and mark its phrase structure directly on the score (this is not included in the Anthology). Then look at the incomplete phrase diagram given in Homework Assignment 4.6 of your workbook; this diagram may or may not reflect your interpretation. Fill in the blanks with formal labels (e.g. exposition, primary theme, bridge, etc.), cadence types, measure numbers or key areas, as appropriate. Then answer the questions that follow the diagram.

Homework Assignment 4.7

Choose a movement in sonata form from a Classical-period instrumental chamber work that is not included in the Anthology. Analyze its form by preparing an annotated score. Label the exposition, the development, the recapitulation, each part of the exposition and recapitulation, and all key areas on the score. Finally, write a one-page essay summarizing how it differs from the formal model given in this chapter (see page 55).

Homework Assignment 4.8

Choose a movement in sonata form from a Romantic-period instrumental chamber work that is not included in the Anthology. Analyze its form by preparing an annotated score. Label the exposition, the development, the recapitulation, each part of the exposition and recapitulation, and all key areas on the score. Finally, write a one-page essay summarizing how it differs from the formal model given in this chapter (see page 55).

Homework Assignment 4.9

Write a 1–2 page essay comparing rounded binary form and ternary form with sonata form.

Chapter Review

1   A **sonata form** has three large sections: the *exposition*, the *development*, and the *recapitulation*. The **exposition** is the first section, in which the most important themes of the movement are presented. The **development** is the second section, in which the themes from the exposition are developed. The **recapitulation** is the last section, and is a varied repetition of the exposition.

2   There is one important element that makes sonata form unique: a tonal tension between the primary key and its dominant or relative major in the exposition, a tension that is resolved in the recapitulation.

3   Expositions can be understood as having four parts, presented in the following order: a *primary theme* (or *theme group*), a *bridge*, a *secondary theme* (or *theme group*), and a *closing*. In major-mode sonata forms, the secondary theme (or theme group) is in the key of the dominant; in minor-mode sonata forms, it is either in the key of the dominant or in the key of the relative major.

4   Development sections are so named because they primarily develop material from the exposition, though occasionally one finds a genuinely new theme there. The primary methods for developing materials in a development section are motivic

repetition (often varied repetition) and sequences (both melodic and harmonic). Often development sections are tonally unstable, with frequent modulations; the passages in keys most distantly related to the primary key are generally found there. Also, they often end on a dominant pedal in the primary key.

5   The recapitulation is a varied repetition of the exposition, and thus can also be understood as having the same four parts, presented in the same order: *primary theme* (or *theme group*), *bridge, secondary theme* (or *theme group*), *closing*. The main difference between the recapitulation and the exposition is that in the recapitulation, the secondary theme is transposed to the primary key, thus resolving the tonal tension between primary and secondary key areas that is found in the exposition.

6   Introductions and codas are never considered "part of" the standard musical forms, but are always options for the composer; movements in sonata form can be preceded by an introduction before the sonata form itself begins, and can conclude with a coda that begins after the sonata form itself is over.

7   In the Classical and Romantic periods, composers writing four-movement sonatas, symphonies, and string quartets typically began with a fast-paced first movement in sonata form and in the primary key. This was usually followed by a slow-paced second movement in a contrasting key that could be in sonata form, though many other forms were commonly used as well. In the Classical period, the third movement was usually a medium-paced Minuet and Trio in triple meter and in the primary key; in the Romantic, it became a fast-paced Scherzo and Trio movement in triple meter, sometimes in the primary key but sometimes in a contrasting key. In both cases, the overall form of the third movement was composite ternary (Minuet-Trio-Minuet or Scherzo-Trio-Scherzo). (Note that sometimes the second and third movements sound like they are reversed: the second movement is a fast scherzo and trio, while the third movement is the slowest movement.) The final movement was usually a fast rondo, sonata-rondo, or sonata form, and was always in the primary key.

chapter 5

Variation Forms

When musicians say that some musical motive, phrase, or section is a variation of another, they mean that it is changed, but not to such an extent that its relation to the original is unrecognizable. Within the context of phrase structure, this idea of variation is bound to the definition of the parallel period (its two phrases begin in the same way but have different endings) and to the definition of the sentence (the second half develops motivic material from the first half through variation). Within the context of sonata form, the development and recapitulation both depend on variation for their definitions, though in strikingly different ways. This chapter will focus on entire forms that depend upon variation for their definition.

Continuous Variations

There are two kinds of variation forms: *sectional variations* and *continuous variations*. The use of the terms "sectional" and "continuous" to describe variation forms is different from the use of those same terms in describing binary forms, though the usage is closely related. They are related in a general way because in both cases "sectional" implies a stronger division between parts while "continuous" implies that the first part could not stand on its own as an independent musical entity. **Continuous variations** are variations in which a relatively short repeated bass line and/or harmonic progression (i.e. generally enough to harmonize one or two phrases of music) is repeated continuously while the melodic material changes each time. Such pieces have been called by many names throughout history: the most common of these names are *ground bass* (or *ostinato bass*), *chaconne*, and *passacaglia*. Both the passacaglia and the chaconne are typically in a slow triple meter and in the minor mode. Though scholars have often argued that the names imply subtly different kinds of pieces, for our purposes it is most useful to think of them as synonymous with the term *continuous variations*. The repeated bass line is often called an *ostinato*, which more generally means a repeated melodic figure.

"Crucifixus" from Bach's *Mass in B Minor* is an example of a ground bass (i.e. a continuous variations form); listen to it while following along with the score (see Anthology, pp. 20–23).

Note that the repetition of the bass line or chord progression does not mean that the phrase structure is equally repetitive. Because phrase endings are defined by the conjunction of melodic and harmonic closure, composers can write the melodic material to emphasize different places within the repetitive structure, and consequently to have a variety of cadence types and phrase lengths. For example, consider the first four cadences in the "Crucifixus": they are an IAC (m. 5), two PACs (mm. 9 and 13), and a HC (m. 16).

In-Class Activity 5.1

Diagram the phrase structure of Bach's "Crucifixus."

In More Detail: Overlapping Phrases

In polyphonic music, it is common to have phrases beginning and ending independently throughout the texture. Such is the case in mm. 13–25 in the "Crucifixus" from Bach's *Mass in B Minor*; listen to this passage while following along with the score (see Anthology, p. 21).

While the four vocal parts in mm. 5–13 can be seen as working together, each contributing a portion of a single phrase, they become more independent after that point. The soprano and bass parts end with a half cadence in m. 16, but the alto and tenor parts push through this cadence point to individual cadences in mm. 18 and 20, respectively. After that, the bass part cadences on its own in m. 23, and the alto cadences on its own in m. 25. The four parts reunite to cadence together in m. 29, marking the end of the first portion of text and preparing for a more homophonic setting of the text that follows.

Sectional Divisions in Continuous Variations

Composers will often add sectional divisions to continuous variations; this is particularly common in vocal music, where a text dictates sectional divisions that do not correspond to the chosen musical form. In such cases one should add upper case letters and brackets to indicate where these sections begin and end, and how the material of each section relates to the others. In the "Cruxificus," the text suggests a division into two parts, A and B, and this division is reflected by the change from a polyphonic texture to a homophonic one in m. 29. The homophony ends with the end of the text in m. 36, and is followed in m. 37 by a return of the opening text and the polyphonic texture of the first section. However, the melodic material here is completely different from that of the first section and this time it sets the entire text, not ending until all parts join together to cadence in m. 49; thus, a label of C seems more appropriate than A' in describing the section. The final measures of the movement feel like a codetta, simply repeating the last three words, but using them to modulate to the key of the relative major. One might summarize the form of the movement as in Example 5.1.

Introduction	A	B	C	Codetta
mm. 1–5	5–29	29–36	36–49	49–end

EXAMPLE 5.1   Diagram of Bach, *Mass in B Minor*, "Cruxificus".

Though the sectional divisions here do not correspond to a binary or a ternary model, such models can easily be combined with continuous variations and often are. Consider the aria "When I am Laid in Earth" from Purcell's *Dido and Aeneas*; listen to it while following along with the score (see Anthology, pp. 373–375).

The repeated bass line and harmonic progression mark it as continuous variations, but Example 5.2 shows how its sectional divisions also mark it as simple binary.

Introduction	‖: A :‖	B	B	Coda
mm. 1–6	6–16	17–28	29–38	39–end

EXAMPLE 5.2   Diagram of Purcell, *Dido and Aeneas*, "When I am Laid in Earth."

Note that the repeat of the B section in mm. 29–38 is written out, but it is almost a literal repetition of mm. 17–28 (the only written changes are in the violin and viola parts in mm. 28 and 30).

In-Class Activity 5.2

Diagram the phrase structure of Purcell's "When I am Laid in Earth."

Homework Assignment 5.1

The fourth movement of Brahms' Symphony No. 4 is a variations form, but with a strong overlay of sonata form elements. Listen to it with the score (see Anthology, pp. 154–184), and then chart the sections and parts in relation to a sonata form model (e.g. Primary Theme, Bridge, Secondary Theme, etc.) as indicated in Homework Assignment 5.1 of your workbook. Note that this movement is not really in sonata form, but rather is just "sonata-like" (it lacks the characteristic tension between key areas in the exposition and its subsequent resolution in the recapitulation). Nevertheless, label the following parts of sonata form in your graphic representation: introduction, exposition, primary theme, bridge, secondary theme, closing, development, and recapitulation.

Sectional Variations

Sectional variations are those in which a theme is presented and then followed by a series of variations based on the melodic/harmonic framework of the initial theme; such pieces are typically entitled "Theme and Variations," for obvious reasons. Brahms' *Variations on a Theme by Haydn* is an example of sectional variations; listen to it while following along with the score (see Anthology, pp. 116–153). Note how there is a pause between each variation, very much like the kind of pause that one puts in between movements in a multi-movement work; this pause is the normal practice when performing sectional variations, and it certainly helps the listener to keep track of the form.

One useful practice when studying a work in sectional variation form is to create a summary of the whole work in which each variation is compared to the others in a short verbal description. Example 5.3 is such a summary for Brahms' *Variations on a Theme by Haydn*.

Except for the Finale, each variation keeps the rounded binary form of the theme, and this is to be expected. In sectional variations from the Classical period, one expects the

---

Theme—*andante*, 2/4, B♭ major, Sectional Rounded Binary Form

Var. I—a little faster, 2/4, B♭ major, bass pedal on tonic in winds and brass accompanies flowing string parts that set a stream of eighth notes against a stream of eighth-note triplets (in the B section, the bass pedal starts on the dominant)

Var. II—*più vivace*, 2/4, B♭ minor, *pizz.* and staccatos in the strings, dotted figure prominent in the winds

Var. III—*con moto*, B♭ major, varied repeats of each section (i.e. no repeat signs), flowing eighth-note melody in winds, features solos in oboe, clarinet and horn

Var. IV—*andante con moto*, 3/8 time, B♭ minor, varied repeats of each section (i.e. no repeat signs), winds and strings take turns presenting a simplified variation of the melody in eighths and quarters, the Neapolitan is prominent throughout

Var. V—*vivace*, 6/8 time with constant stream of eighth notes, B♭ major, syncopated with lots of *sforzandos*, varied repeats of each section (i.e. no repeat signs), winds and strings take turns presenting primary melody in the A section

Var. VI—*vivace*, 2/4, B♭ major, horns featured, literal repeats return, cadences in A section are in G major (though the primary key is still B♭ major), eighth–sixteenth–sixteenth rhythm featured throughout

Var. VII—*grazioso*, 6/8, B♭ major, *dolce* melody featuring first flute and violas, literal repeats, dotted eighth–sixteenth–eighth rhythm throughout

Var. VIII—*presto non troppo*, 3/4, B♭ minor, soft dynamics throughout, muted strings, starts with violas and cellos alone (first five bars), that material is then inverted and shifted up to the winds (next five bars), a varied repetition of the A section follows, there is a literal repeat of the music after the A section

Finale—*andante*, cut time, B♭ major, a continuous variations on the bass line B♭–B♭–E♭–D–C–B♭–E♭–C–F–F (a synthesis of the theme and the bass line from mm. 1–5)

EXAMPLE 5.3   Summary of Brahms, *Variations on a Theme by Haydn*.

theme to be in some kind of binary or ternary form, and for each variation to be in the same form as the theme. Though Brahms is a Romantic composer, this work is drawing on the Classical model. The Finale, however, departs from that model and uses a continuous variations form, a surprise that could be viewed as Romantic since one would expect the form of the Finale to be the same as that of the theme. Using a different form for the last variation would have been unusual in the Classical period.

A knowledge of historical trends in composition often makes approaching unfamiliar works from the common-practice period easier. Baroque composers wrote far more continuous variations than sectional variations, but in the Classical and Romantic periods, the reverse is true. In sectional variations from the Classical period, the tonic will remain the same for each variation, but at least one variation will be in the parallel minor if the theme is in major, or in the parallel major if the theme is in minor. Again, Brahms is drawing on the Classical model in this set of variations: all of the movements have B♭ as tonic, and there are three variations in minor (the theme is in major).

In-Class Activity 5.3

Listen to Brahms' *Variations on a Theme by Haydn* without the score using the summary provided in Example 5.3. Pause the recording before each variation to read the description, then play it and try to identify each part of the description in the music that you hear.

Homework Assignment 5.2

Listen to Mozart's Piano Sonata, K. 331, I with the score (see Anthology, pp. 276–281), and then summarize the differences between the theme and each subsequent variation in Homework Assignment 5.2 of your workbook, using Example 5.3 as a model.

In More Detail: Phrase Rhythm and Hypermeter

Phrase rhythm is the rhythm of phrase organization, and is understood in terms of *hypermeter*. To understand hypermeter, it makes sense to first review the definition of meter: a meter is a recurring pattern of beat accentuation, and is reflected by the time signature and bar lines in musical notation. For example, pieces in 4/4 time typically have a strong accent on beat 1 (often brought about by a harmonic change), a secondary accent on beat 3, and relatively weak accents on beats 2 and 4. In a similar way, **hypermeter** is a recurring pattern of bar accentuation, usually brought about by the beginnings and endings of phrases. For example, consider the first theme from Mozart's Piano Sonata, K. 331 in Example 5.4.

Sing this theme while conducting, but rather than conducting the meter, conduct the hypermeter indicated above using a slow 4-beat pattern. Like many Classical works,

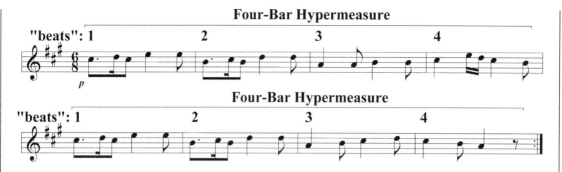

EXAMPLE 5.4 Hypermeter in Mozart's Piano Sonata, K. 331, mm. 1–8.

the symmetrical 4-bar phrasing of Mozart's theme creates a 4-bar hypermeter, and so its phrase rhythm can be understood in terms of a much slower 4-beat pattern. Note, however, that a slow 2-beat hypermeter would also work well for this theme, and would also fit the music after measure 8 better (see Anthology, p. 276). If one continues in the slow four pattern to the end, one is forced to end on "beat 2" of the hypermeter, because there is a 2-bar cadential extension to the final phrase.

Hypermeter has practical performance applications, particularly with meters that are felt in 1 (i.e. one beat per bar). In the Scherzo to his Ninth Symphony, Beethoven marked in the score where he wanted it to be conducted in 4, and where he wanted it to be conducted in 3, and he was clearly intending for hypermeasures to be conducted, since the notated time signature in the movement is 3/4 and it is far too fast to conduct the notated time signature in 3. By conducting hypermeasures, a conductor can indicate not only the tempo of the music, but also how measures are grouped into phrases.

Now listen to and conduct the hypermeasures in Var. VIII of Brahms' *Variations on a Theme by Haydn* using the following guide (see Anthology, pp. 140–141):

mm. 322–341   ‖: mm. 342–345 (hemiolas conducted)
four hypermeasures in 5;   two hypermeasures of 3 (half note = "beat"),

mm. 346–349 (hemiolas conducted)   mm. 350–357
two hypermeasures of 3 (half note = "beat"),   two hypermeasures in 4

mm. 358–end :‖
hypermeasure in 3

Note that the hypermeters in mm. 342–349 reflect hemiolas—the implied 2-beat patterns—rather than the notated meter. Just like the beat seems to speed up in m. 342 and then slow down in m. 350, your beat pattern should speed up and slow down in those two spots. In performance, a conductor might choose to simply conduct in 1 over the hemiolas, since conducting the implied meter makes it harder for those counting rests to keep their places; however, if one does so, the beats in that section will feel syncopated because of the hemiolas.

The Blues

As a musical term, "blues" has two meanings. The first is a more general reference to the character of a piece: it is harmonically simple (i.e. there are few harmonies and no modulations), and it features the "blues third" melodically, which is a minor third above the root when the harmony below has a major third above the root. The second meaning is more specific, referring to a kind of continuous variation form with the harmonic structure I | I | I | I | IV | IV | I | I | V | IV | I | I (to distinguish between the two meanings, musicians will often call it "the 12-bar blues," since the repeated harmonic structure is twelve bars long). Each 12-bar unit typically sets three 4-bar melodic phrases; the three phrases are structured as *a a b*, with the first two phrases named "the call," and the final phrase named "the response." Each 12-bar unit is called a "chorus" and the lyrics for a blues typically change for every chorus, though the melody is often the same (note how the term "chorus" is used here as it was in the discussion of the 32-bar song form in Chapter 3, not the way it is used in pop and rock music).

EXAMPLE 5.5 The structure of the 12-bar blues.

Improvisation is also an important part of the blues, and improvisations are built around the structure of the chorus. A musician improvising on the blues will start improvising at the beginning of a chorus, improvise over one or more choruses, and end their improvisation at the end of a chorus, so that the melody might be played or sung again, or so that another musician might begin an improvisation. Thus, it is essential to keep track of the 12-bar cycle when playing the blues, and to fully appreciate it, it is just as important to keep track of the cycle when listening to one.

In-Class Activity 5.4

Listen to B.B. King playing "Stormy Monday" and to Stevie Ray Vaughn playing "Pride and Joy"; while listening to each of these performances, conduct along in 4 and count off the measures in the 12-bar structure, cueing the beginning of each chorus with the other hand.

Form in Jazz

Music in jazz can be categorized in many different ways, but one useful way is to differentiate between jazz compositions written to be performed in a jazz style with substantive improvisations, and what jazz musicians typically call "standards"—music written and made popular in another style, and subsequently performed in a jazz style. One of the most popular sources for standards are songs from the first half of the twentieth century by composers such as George Gershwin, Cole Porter, Irving Berlin, Jerome Kern, and Richard Rogers and thus many are in the 32-bar song form. However, when these are performed by jazz musicians, the harmonic structure of the tune becomes a vehicle for improvisation in a way very similar to how the 12-bar blues is treated by improvisers: the music is clearly divided into multiple choruses, all of which have the same harmonic structure as the original body of the tune.

In a typical jazz performance, the melody (often called the "head" by jazz musicians) is played during the first and last of these choruses, and in the middle the musicians take turns improvising over one or more choruses. Each improvisation begins with the beginning of a chorus and ends with the end of a chorus, but how many choruses are taken by a soloist is often left up to them. Drum solos present the only exception to this formula. Though sometimes drum soloists do take entire choruses, it is also common for the ensemble to "trade fours" with the drummer: the chorus is divided up into four-measure blocks, and there is a regular alternation between four measures of the full ensemble accompanying a melodic soloist, and four measures of drum solo.

There is a close relationship between continuous variations in the Baroque, Classical, and Romantic periods, and the blues and jazz in performance: in all these styles, there is a regularly recurring harmonic progression underpinning melodic material that is constantly changing above it. However, continuous variations that are found in the Baroque, Classical, and Romantic periods typically set only one or two phrases of music, while the 12-bar blues sets three phrases, and jazz compositions and jazz standards often set more than three (the 32-bar song form typically sets eight). Nevertheless, the listening strategy is to a large extent the same for continuous variations, the blues, and jazz: one must keep track of where one is relative to the repeated harmonic structure in order to fully appreciate the form.

In-Class Activity 5.5

Listen to the Miles Davis Quintet playing "Four"; while listening to the performance, count off the measures of the 32-bar form in groups of eight with your fingers (ABAB'; it's in 4/4 time and the bass line mostly "walks" with a seldom-interrupted stream of quarter notes). Clap once to cue the beginning of each chorus.

Homework Assignment 5.3

Go online and download one of the following jazz performances: 1) Miles Davis (trumpet) playing "Just Squeeze Me" (album: *The Legendary Prestige Quintet Sessions*); 2) Bill Evans (piano) playing "Wrap Your Troubles in Dreams" (album: *Interplay*); 3) John Coltrane (tenor sax) playing "I Hear a Rhapsody" (album: *Lush Life*). Listen to the performance you choose and then chart what happens in each chorus of the 32-bar song form in Homework Assignment 5.3 of your workbook.

Homework Assignment 5.4

Choose a Baroque, Classical, or Romantic period instrumental chamber work that is in a continuous variations form and is not included in the Anthology. Analyze its form, phrase structure, key areas, and harmonic sequences by preparing an annotated score. Bracket each iteration of the ostinato bass and label sections of the form if there are sectional divisions (see pp. 64–65). To show its phrase structure, mark each phrase ending where it occurs with the cadence type below the system and each subphrase ending with a comma above the system.

Homework Assignment 5.5

Write a 1–2 page essay about a Baroque, Classical, or Romantic period instrumental chamber work that is in a sectional variations form and is not included in the Anthology. Summarize the differences between the theme and each subsequent variation using Example 5.3 as a model (see page 66).

Chapter Review

1   **Continuous variations** are variations in which a relatively short repeated bass line and/or harmonic progression (i.e. generally enough to harmonize one or two phrases of music) is repeated continuously while the melodic material changes each time. Such pieces have been called by many names throughout history, with the most common being *ground bass, chaconne*, and *passacaglia*. Both the passacaglia and the chaconne are typically in a slow triple meter and in the minor mode.

2   **Sectional variations** are those in which a theme is presented and then followed by a series of variations based on the melodic/harmonic framework of the initial theme; such pieces are typically entitled "Theme and Variations." In performance, there is a pause between each variation, very much like the kind of pause that one puts in between movements in a multi-movement work.

3   Baroque composers wrote far more continuous variations than sectional variations, but in the Classical and Romantic periods, the reverse is true.

4   In sectional variations from the Classical period, one can expect each variation to be in the same form as the theme (binary or ternary). One can also expect that the tonic will remain the same for each variation, but that at least one variation will be

in the parallel minor if the theme is in major, or in the parallel major if the theme is in minor.

5   As a musical form, the **12-bar blues** is a kind of continuous variation form with the harmonic structure I | I | I | I | IV | IV | I | I | V | IV | I | I. A musician improvising on the blues will start improvising at the beginning of a chorus, improvise over one or more choruses, and end their improvisation at the end of a chorus, so that the melody might be played or sung again, or so that another musician might begin an improvisation.

6   In jazz, the harmonic structure of the tune becomes a vehicle for improvisation in a way very similar to how the 12-bar blues is treated by improvisers: the music is clearly divided into multiple choruses, all of which have the same harmonic structure as the original body of the tune.

chapter 6

Imitative Forms

Imitation is the repetition of a motive or a melodic fragment in another voice. There are three kinds of pieces that use imitation as the primary basis of composition: *canons*, *inventions*, and *fugues*. There is a debate among musicians as to whether these kinds of pieces should be called "forms" or whether they should be called "compositional processes." They are called "imitative forms" here, but only reluctantly, since they are unlike the other forms that have been discussed so far. They do not divide neatly into sections, like binary and ternary forms do. The kind of ambiguity that makes distinguishing the beginnings and endings of the smaller parts of a sonata form exposition—the primary theme, the bridge, the second theme, and the closing—is everywhere in the imitative forms, and there are no larger divisions consistently found in the imitative forms like those separating the exposition, development, and recapitulation in a sonata form. Nevertheless, if one considers musical form a way of understanding large-scale repetition, variation, and development in a work, then the term "form" still seems appropriate. Canons, inventions, and fugues are not devoid of form after all, and the sense of order in these imitative forms goes beyond just their common use of imitation as a compositional technique.

Canon

A **canon** is the strictest kind of imitative writing, in which every voice that enters after the first imitates the first note-for-note, only breaking the imitation at cadence points. The first voice in a canon is called the **dux** (Latin for "leader"), while the second voice that enters is called the **comes** (Latin for "follower"). Canons are undoubtedly the imitative form that most people encounter first in their lives: "Row, Row, Row Your Boat" and "Frère Jacques" are both canons. Canons, however, are by no means limited to child-like simplicity; a virtuosic demonstration of canonic possibilities is found in Bach's *Goldberg Variations*, where he systematically explores canons at the unison, second, third, fourth, fifth, sixth, seventh, octave, and ninth (in a canon at the second, the *comes* would enter a second higher than the *dux* and would continue with all of its corresponding notes being a step higher; in a canon at the third, the *comes* would enter a third higher, etc.).

Invention

An **invention** is a shorter imitative work in two or three parts by J. S. Bach. It might at first seem odd to dedicate a whole section of a textbook to a type of composition that was written by only one composer, but it is justified here because of the extent to which the music of Bach in general and the inventions in particular have been influential to musicians since Bach's time, even up until the present day. Example 6.1 diagrams the phrase structure of Bach's Two-Part Invention No. 1.

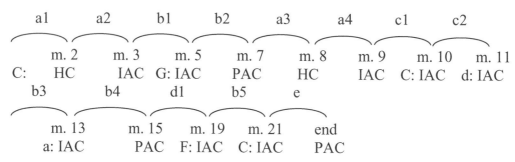

EXAMPLE 6.1   Phrase Diagram of Bach's Two-Part Invention No. 1.

Listen to a recording of this invention and compare this phrase diagram with the music (see Anthology, p. 2). The main melodic material of this invention is contained entirely within the right-hand part of the first measure; every other measure in the invention can be directly related to it. This explains the interpretation of the phrase structure given in Example 6.1: the main melodic material is considered to be an independent musical idea and so the first cadence is taken at the conclusion of that idea, the downbeat of m. 2. Another equally valid interpretation might consider the main melodic material in the right hand of m. 1 to be a subphrase, and would group together what are labeled as a1 and a2 above into a single phrase (such an interpretation would consequently view some of the other phrases in Example 6.1 as subphrases in a similar way, and group them accordingly). Notice that similar letters are used to reflect a transposition of material: a3 and a4 (mm. 7–8) use almost the same material as a1 and a2 (mm. 1–2), but transposed to begin on the dominant pitch and with the roles of the left and right hands reversed. Also, b3 and b4 (mm. 11–14) use almost the same material as b1 and b2 (mm. 3–6), but transposed and modally inflected to begin in D minor rather than C major, and again with the roles of the left and right hands reversed. Two-part counterpoint such as this, that works regardless of which voice is on top, is called **invertible counterpoint** and is often found in imitative works.

Development in Imitative Forms

Immediately after the main melodic material is presented in an imitative form, that material begins to be developed, and it continues to be developed until the very end. The most common developmental technique used in imitative forms is to take motives from the first few measures and build sequences with them. Another commonly used technique is **inversion**, a melodic variation in which the direction of each interval is reversed (e.g. if the motive starts by skipping up a third and then moves down by step twice, its inversion will start by skipping down a third and then moves up by step twice). Example 6.2 illustrates how the sequence in mm. 3–4 of Bach's Two-Part Invention No. 1 is built from inversions of the head motive in m. 1.

EXAMPLE 6.2   Inversional relationship between m. 1 and mm. 3–4.

The head motive and its inversion are the building blocks for every sequence in this invention, though each sequence uses them in a different way.

There are three developmental rhythmic techniques that one will often find in imitative forms: *augmentation, diminution,* and *stretto*. **Augmentation** is a melodic variation in which the duration of each note is doubled, while **diminution** is a melodic variation in which the duration of each note is halved. Examples of both augmentation and diminution can be found in Beethoven's String Quartet, Op. 131, I; as shown in Example 6.3 (for full score, see Anthology, pp. 113–115).

a) Main melodic material of the fugue, mm. 1–4.

b) Head motive in diminution, m. 54.

c) Main melodic material in augmentation, mm. 99–107.

EXAMPLE 6.3   Augmentation and Diminution in Beethoven's Op. 131, I.

The very first four notes (mm. 1–2) are a head motive that is developed throughout. It is played in diminution by the first violin part starting with the pick up to m. 54 (this instance is in a different key as well). The first four measures of this movement provide the main melodic material for the entire movement, and are played in augmentation by the cello in mm. 99–107 (the first and last notes are adjusted to fit the new context, but other than those notes it is a faithful augmentation played two octaves lower).

In **stretto**, melodic material enters in one voice, then enters in another voice before the first voice has completed its statement of the material, thus creating an overlap. In stretto, there is a sense of rhythmic acceleration because there is a shorter time interval between successive entries than there would be if there were no such overlap. Examples of stretto are easy to find in Bach's F Major Fugue from the *Well-Tempered Clavier*, Book I (see Anthology, pp. 5–6): the main melodic material (mm. 1–4) is four measures long, but in m. 28 an entry in the right hand overlaps an entry in the bass by entering just two measures afterward, and in mm. 37–44 and mm. 47–54, similar overlaps are found.

In-Class Activity 6.1

Listen to Bach's Two-Part Invention No. 1 in C major (see Anthology, p. 2) and analyze its motivic structure directly on the score by bracketing every melodic fragment based on the head motive (the first seven notes of the invention) as "x" and every melodic fragment based on the tail motive (the next four notes) as "y." Compare your answers with other students in your class.

Homework Assignment 6.1

Listen to J. S. Bach's Two-Part Invention No. 13 in A Minor while following along with the score (see Anthology, p. 3), and mark cadence points in the score as you listen. Then look at the incomplete phrase diagram in Homework Assignment 6.1 of your workbook; this diagram may or may not reflect your interpretation. Fill in the blanks with cadence types, sequence types, measure numbers or key areas, as appropriate.

Fugue

A fugue is an imitative work in three or more voices that begins with a **subject**, the primary thematic material for the work, being presented successively by each voice in turn. When all the voices have entered, there is an **episode**, in which material from the subject is developed by all of the voices in a freely contrapuntal texture until there is a **restatement**, in which the subject in its entirety is again presented in one or more voices, after which there is a regular alternation of episodes and restatements until the end of the fugue. The subject entries in an exposition typically alternate between presentations of the subject in the tonic key and presentations that are either transposed to the key of the dominant or presented at the level of the dominant—these latter kind of entries are called **answers**. The diagram in Formal Model 6.1 summarizes the parts of a fugue.

Exposition	Episode	(followed by an alternation of
S enters, followed by **A**, followed by an alternation of S and A entries until all voices have entered	sequences and motivic development	Restatements and Episodes in various closely related keys until the music returns to the tonic key and the fugue ends)

S = Subject, A = Answer, Restatement = return of the subject in its entirety

FORMAL MODEL 6.1 Fugue.

Example 6.4 shows how Bach realizes this model in one of his fugues.

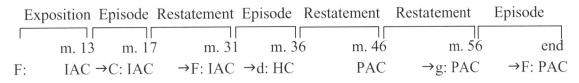

Exposition Episode Restatement Episode Restatement Restatement Episode

    m. 13   m. 17   m. 31   m. 36   m. 46   m. 56   end

F: IAC →C: IAC   →F: IAC →d: HC   PAC   →g: PAC →F: PAC

EXAMPLE 6.4 Diagram of Fugue in F Major, *Well-Tempered Clavier*, Book I.

Compare this diagram to the music (see Anthology, pp. 5–6). In this particular fugue, all three voices present the subject or answer in their entirety not just in the exposition (which one would expect in any fugue), but in each restatement as well. Take the time to find all of these entries (you should find thirteen in mm. 1–56). It is important to note that, in order to have a fugal restatement, you only need to have the fugal subject presented in one voice; the fact that Bach has all three voices present the subject or answer in each restatement is one of the things that adds to the individuality of this particular fugue, but it is not a feature that one should expect to find in others. (Another interpretation of this music is to have a final restatement beginning in m. 65; the top voice at that point begins what could easily be interpreted as an embellished version of the subject.)

Another interesting aspect of this fugue is the fact that it sounds as though there are two restatements presented in succession without the intervening episode that our formal model above would lead us to expect. One could interpret these two restatements as one giant restatement that spans two keys and has six subject entries: three in D minor, followed by three in G minor. However, this interpretation seems to be at odds with how the piece sounds: the cadence in m. 46 is strong, and the fact that *all three* of the voices in the fugue have stated the subject in the same key of D minor, coupled with the fact that the cadence in m. 46 confirms the key of D minor, only underscores the sense of finality. The cadence here sounds like the end of a section, and though the parts of the formal model for fugue do not have to be separated by the kind of sectional boundaries we find in binary and ternary forms, when such boundaries are found in a fugue, they almost always do align with the end of an exposition, episode, or restatement.

Subjects, Answers and Countersubjects in a Fugue

Though subjects vary greatly in length, they are usually one or two phrases of music. Example 6.5 shows two different fugal subjects from Bach's *Well-Tempered Clavier*, Book I. The first one in C♯ minor is extremely short, consisting of just five notes, while the second one in B♭ major is relatively long (note that each subphrase of the B♭ major subject has more notes in it than the entire C♯ minor subject!).

a) Subject from Fugue in C♯ Minor.

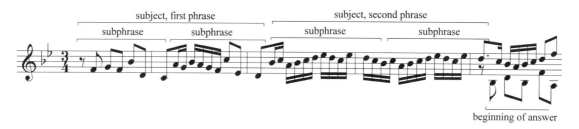

b) Subject from Fugue in B♭ Major.

EXAMPLE 6.5   Two fugal subjects from Bach's *Well-Tempered Clavier*, Book I.

Musicians have historically made a distinction between two different types of answers: *tonal answers* and *real answers*. A **tonal answer** is a "tonally adjusted" version of the subject at the level of the dominant (that is, the key does not necessarily change, but the scale-degree pattern of the subject is for the most part shifted to be a fifth higher or some octave equivalent of that relationship: $\hat{1}$ becomes $\hat{5}$, $\hat{2}$ becomes $\hat{6}$, etc.). One should note, however, that a single change to the scale-degree pattern of the subject is often made to suit the harmony in a tonal answer: though the single change made could be a variety of different things, it is usually that $\hat{5}$ in the subject is answered by $\hat{1}$ rather than the scale-degree a fifth higher (which would be $\hat{2}$). A **real answer** is an exact transposition of the subject to the key of the dominant. Example 6.6 illustrates the answers to each of the fugal subjects given in Example 6.5, respectively, that are found in the fugues.

a) Real answer from Fugue in C♯ Minor.

EXAMPLE 6.6   Two fugal answers from Bach's *Well-Tempered Clavier*, Book I.

tonal answer

b) Tonal answer from Fugue in B♭ Major.

EXAMPLE 6.6 continued

Observe how the answer from Bach's C♯ Minor Fugue (see Example 6.6a) is an exact transposition of that fugue's subject (see Example 6.5a), while in the answer from Bach's B♭ Major Fugue (see Example 6.6b), the first and third notes of the answer are a step lower than they would be if transposed to the key of the dominant (compare Example 6.5b to Example 6.6b).

Some fugues have a **countersubject**, which is an accompaniment to the subject that returns to accompany each time the subject or its answer returns. It is just as long as the subject and occurs simultaneously with it in almost all presentations after the first (in the first, the subject is heard alone). The pitch level at which a countersubject returns doesn't matter; if the same accompaniment returns consistently each time the subject or answer returns, it is called a countersubject. Example 6.7 shows the first two counter-subjects in Bach's Fugue in F Major, from the *Well-Tempered Clavier*, Book I.

answer   countersubject

countersubject

subject

EXAMPLE 6.7 Bach, *Well-Tempered Clavier*, Book I, Fugue in F Major, mm. 5–13.

What if the subject appears in some key other than the dominant? Is it called the answer or the subject? If the melodic material associated with the subject occurs in any other key, it is simply called the subject, despite the fact that some of these entries at other pitch levels might seem to be more related to the answer than the subject (e.g. even if the adjustment made to a tonal answer is found in the new key, it is called the subject).

Hearing Fugues

While listening to a fugue or fugato, you should constantly be shifting your attention to follow the voice that is currently presenting the subject or answer, and in rehearsal or performance, performers should always strive to make these shifts of attention easy for the audience—this is usually accomplished by balancing the parts dynamically as one would when the main theme shifts to the bass or to an inner part. (This same idea should also be applied to the performance of inventions.) One common way of rehearsing fugues and fugatos is to have the performers only play their parts when they have the subject or answer, and to stop playing as soon as the subject or answer is over. The effect makes all the performers very aware of who should sound like the leader at any given point in the performance, and then performers can gauge their own dynamic levels throughout based on whether or not they can hear the leader's part.

In-Class Activity 6.2

Listen to Bach's Fugue in F Major from his *Well-Tempered Clavier*, Book I (see Anthology, pp. 5–6) and mark its phrase structure directly on the score. Compare your answers with other students in your class.

Homework Assignment 6.2

Listen to Bach's Fugue in E minor from his *Well-Tempered Clavier*, Book II with the score (see Anthology, pp. 9–12), then label all subjects, answers, and countersubjects on the score and add brackets that indicate both the beginning and the ending of each, marking them in such a way as to make clear the "voice" (soprano, alto, tenor, bass) that carries it (e.g. "Sub. in Bass," "Real Ans. in Alto," "C. S. in Tenor," etc.). Sometimes the countersubject will be broken between two voices, in which case you should use arrows to show how and where the statement is passed off and continued in another voice. Next, mark all harmonic sequences with brackets (again mark both the beginning and the ending) and label them by type (e.g. $\downarrow$5 seq., #2 seq., etc.). Don't bother marking melodic sequences that are not accompanied by a harmonic sequence, or using the labels "exposition," "episode," and "restatement"; there will be enough annotations as it is.

Difficulties in Analyzing Fugues

There are a number of things that make analyzing a fugue difficult. First, it is sometimes difficult to determine the implied cadence at the end of the first presentation of the subject, because at that point it is unharmonized. In general, one can take endings on $\hat{1}$ to suggest PACs, endings on $\hat{3}$ to suggest IACs, and endings on $\hat{2}$ or $\hat{7}$ to suggest HCs. However, what about endings on $\hat{5}$? And what about endings where the sense of melodic closure seems to come after the sense of harmonic closure? Decisions about implied harmonies are often difficult, and the details of each particular fugue should always be used to make an informed choice. Fortunately, in difficult cases, the notes leading to the ending can often help to clarify the role of the subject's last note through their own harmonic implications.

Second, it is often difficult to decide on exactly where the subject ends and the counter-subject begins, which of course would make determining the cadence difficult. For example, in Bach's Fugue in F Major, most musicians would agree that the subject either ends in m. 4 or m. 5 because the answer begins with the pickup to m. 5, but many would disagree about the exact location. Example 6.8 shows the beginning of this fugue up to the entrance of the answer. There are three reasonable choices, which are marked in the example: a) the downbeat of m. 4; b) beat 2 of m. 4; or c) the downbeat of m. 5.

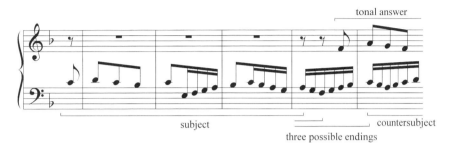

EXAMPLE 6.8   Bach, *Well-Tempered Clavier*, Book I, Fugue in F Major, mm. 1–5.

One cannot definitively say which is right, but something that should be considered when making such a decision is how the end of the subject is treated in each restatement. Out of all the restatements, only one of them actually sticks to the original ending of the subject if we take that ending to be on the downbeat of m. 5; however, even this does not discount the possibility of our third choice, because one could simply argue that the very end of the subject in the restatements is varied each time. Where the subject ends is usually a matter of interpretation, subject to personal opinion, but it is important to have an opinion, because it can determine where you place the very first cadence in performance, not to mention most of the cadences after that in any given fugue.

Finally, it is sometimes hard to decide how much free counterpoint between subject entries constitutes an episode, since it is common to have a measure or two of free counterpoint in between subject and answer entries in the exposition (e.g. see m. 9 in Example 6.7), and this practice can be found in restatements with multiple entries as well.

In-Class Activity 6.3

Listen to the first movement of Beethoven's String Quartet Op. 131 with the score (see Anthology, pp. 113–115) and answer the following questions:

1 This movement is obviously a fugue, but what form would one expect in a first movement from a Classical composer?
2 How does the exposition of this fugue differ from the model?
3 Where are the Restatements in this fugue?
4 How many descending fifth sequences can you find on the first page of the score, and where are they?
5 What type of harmonic sequence is heard in mm. 50–53?
6 What is particularly Romantic about the harmony and voice leading in mm. 107–121 (the end)?

Then analyze the motivic structure of this movement by bracketing every melodic fragment based on the head motive (the first four notes of the subject) as "x" and every melodic fragment based on the tail motive (the rest of the subject after the fourth note) as "y."

Homework Assignment 6.3

Listen to J. S. Bach's Fugue in B Major from his *The Well-Tempered Clavier*, Book I while following along with the score (see Anthology, pp. 7–8), and mark cadence points in the score as you listen. Then look at the incomplete phrase diagram of the fugue in Homework Assignment 6.3 of your workbook; this diagram may or may not reflect your interpretation. Fill in the blanks with formal labels (e.g. exposition, episode, etc.), cadence types, sequence types, measure numbers or key areas, as appropriate (blanks before colons are for keys). Be sure to distinguish between real and tonal answers in the appropriate blanks.

Fugato

A fugue-like section of a movement or work is called a **fugato**. Fugatos are often found in the development sections of sonata forms and sonata-rondos, though they are not so common that one should expect a development section to have one. Because it is not really a fugue, one cannot necessarily expect anything more than an exposition-like set of imitative entries, though fugatos sometimes do follow the model of a fugue in a fairly rigorous way. Compare the fugato from the fourth movement of Haydn's Symphony No. 101 (see Anthology, pp. 252–254) to Example 6.9.

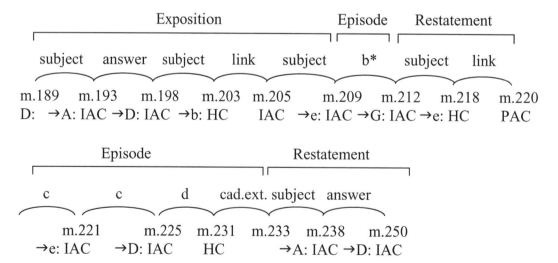

* Phrase letters above begin with "b" because all subjects and answers would be interpreted as some form of "a" if we had used letters to label them instead.

EXAMPLE 6.9   Diagram of fugato from Haydn, Symphony No. 101, IV.

Observe two differences between the exposition here and a true fugal exposition: 1) the first subject entry is accompanied by a countersubject rather than presented alone; and 2) the final subject entry in the exposition at m. 205 is in the key of B minor (the submediant) rather than in the key of either the tonic or the dominant. Despite these two differences, this fugato is pretty faithful to the fugal model given earlier. Note also how each of the two episodes, while linked to the end of the previous section through elision, is at the same time given the character of an episode because each one travels through a descending fifth sequence.

Homework Assignment 6.4

Listen to the fugue from the overture to Handel's *Messiah* while following along with the score (see Anthology, pp. 226–229), and mark cadence points in the score as you listen. Then look at the incomplete phrase diagram of the fugue on page 39 of your workbook; this diagram may or may not reflect your interpretation. Fill in the blanks with formal labels (e.g. exposition, episode, etc.), cadence types, sequence types, measure numbers or key areas, as appropriate (blanks before colons are for keys). Be sure to distinguish between real and tonal answers in the appropriate blanks.

Homework Assignment 6.5

Listen to Bach's Fugue in G minor from his *Well-Tempered Clavier*, Book I with the score (not included in the Anthology), and then mark all subjects, answers, and countersubjects on the score using brackets that indicate both the beginning and the ending of each one, and placing them in such a way as to make clear the "voice" (soprano, alto, tenor, bass) that carries each one. Next, find a clear harmonic sequence, mark it with brackets (mark both the beginning and the ending) and label it by type (e.g. ↓5 seq., #2 seq., etc.). Don't bother marking melodic sequences that are not accompanied by a harmonic sequence; they are obvious enough as they are.

Homework Assignment 6.6

Listen to the fugato (mm. 183–214) from the second movement of Beethoven's Symphony No. 7 with the score (not included in the Anthology), and then mark all subjects, answers, and countersubjects on the score using brackets that indicate both the beginning and the ending of each one, and placing them in such a way as to make clear the "voice" (soprano, alto, tenor, bass) that carries each one. Next, find a clear harmonic sequence, mark it with brackets (mark both the beginning and the ending) and label it by type (e.g. ↓5 seq., #2 seq., etc.). Don't bother marking melodic sequences that are not accompanied by a harmonic sequence; they are obvious enough as they are.

Homework Assignment 6.7

Choose a fugue from a Baroque, Classical or Romantic-period instrumental chamber work that is not included in the Anthology and analyze its form by preparing an annotated score. Label its exposition, episodes, restatements, key areas, and harmonic sequences by type on the score.

Homework Assignment 6.8

Choose a fugato from a Baroque, Classical or Romantic-period choral work that is not included in the Anthology and analyze its form by preparing an annotated score. Label its exposition, episodes, restatements, key areas, and harmonic sequences by type on the score. Finally, write a one-page essay that describes how this fugato differs from what one would expect of a fugue.

Homework Assignment 6.9

Write a 1–2 page essay comparing the structure of a fugue to that of a dramatic dialogue in a play or film.

Chapter Review

1 **Imitation** is the repetition of a motive or a melodic fragment in another voice. There are three kinds of pieces that use imitation as the primary basis of composition: *canons*, *inventions*, and *fugues*.

2 A **canon** is the strictest kind of imitative writing, in which every voice that enters after the first imitates the first note-for-note, only breaking the imitation at cadence points. The first voice in a canon is called the *dux* (Latin for "leader"), while the second voice that enters is called the **comes** (Latin for "follower").

3 An **invention** is a shorter imitative work in two or three parts by J. S. Bach.

4 A **fugue** is an imitative work in three or more voices that begins with a **subject**, the primary thematic material for the work, being presented successively by each voice in turn. When all the voices have entered, there is an **episode**, in which material from the subject is developed by all of the voices in a freely contrapuntal texture until there is a **restatement**, in which the subject in its entirety is again presented in one or more voices. Then there is a regular alternation of episodes and restatements until the end of the fugue.

5 The opening part of a fugue is called the **exposition**. It begins with just a single voice presenting the subject, after which the rest of the voices join the first one by

one, each presenting the subject as it enters, the texture building with each new entry. As each new voice enters with the subject, the voice that had the subject previously switches to accompanimental material. The subject entries in an exposition typically alternate between presentations of the subject in the tonic key, and those that are either transposed to the key of the dominant or presented at the level of the dominant—these latter kind of entries are called **answers**.

6 The **subject** of a fugue is its primary thematic material upon which the entire fugue is based. The **answer** of a fugue is the name given to the subject when it is either transposed to the key of the dominant or presented at the level of the dominant. An exact transposition to the key of the dominant is called a *real answer*, while a "tonally adjusted" version at the level of the dominant is called a *tonal answer*.

7 An **episode** in a fugue is a part in which material from the subject is developed by all of the voices in a freely contrapuntal texture, often through the use of sequences.

8 A **restatement** in a fugue is a part after the initial exposition in which the subject in its entirety is again presented in one or more voices.

9 A **countersubject** in a fugue is an accompaniment to the subject that returns to accompany each time the subject or its answer returns. A countersubject is just as long as the subject and occurs simultaneously with it in almost all presentations after the first (in the first, the subject is heard alone). The pitch level at which a countersubject returns doesn't matter; if the same accompaniment returns consistently each time the subject or answer returns, it is called a countersubject.

10 A **fugato** is a fugue-like section of a movement or work. Fugatos are often found in the development sections of sonata forms and sonata-rondos, though they are not so common that one should expect a development section to have one.

11 Some common developmental techniques often found in imitative forms are *inversion*, *stretto*, *augmentation*, and *diminution*. **Inversion** is a melodic variation in which the direction of each interval is reversed. **Stretto** is the technique of writing overlapping subject entries. **Augmentation** is a melodic variation in which the duration of each note is doubled, and **diminution** is a melodic variation in which the duration of each note is halved.

chapter 7

Concerto Forms

All concerto forms feature soloists and depend upon the juxtaposition of those soloists with the larger group that accompanies them. There is a great variety among concerto forms. Some have just a single soloist, while others have two or more. Some seem to follow a formal model rather strictly, while others can hardly be related to any model. Those from the Classical and Romantic periods involve elements of sonata form, but those from the Baroque do not. However, the juxtaposition between soloists and the full ensemble is common to all concerto forms. In concerto forms, the thematic presentations are often given to the full ensemble, while the developmental material is often given to the soloists, and it is the regular alternation between thematic presentations and developmental material that allows a useful comparison with fugues. In fugues, there is also a regular alternation between thematic presentations and developmental material. In fugues, the thematic presentations are always some form of the subject, while in concerto forms the thematic presentations may not always be of the same material. In fugues, the developmental parts of the form are not associated with any particular voice in the ensemble, while in concerto forms, these developmental parts typically feature the soloists. Nevertheless, recognizing the regular alternation between thematic presentation and developmental material in each makes them both easier to follow.

Ritornello Form

A **ritornello** is a passage featuring the whole ensemble (literally, it means "return"), and a regular alternation between ritornellos and solo sections throughout an entire movement is called **ritornello form**. Movements in ritornello form are common in the first and last movements of Baroque concertos. The ritornellos are passages that feature the larger ensemble, while the solo sections feature the soloist(s). While a ritornello usually presents thematic material, a **solo section** often develops motives from the ritornellos.

Opening Ritornello	Solo Section	(followed by an alternation of
Ritornello theme presented by full ensemble in the tonic key	sequences and motivic development featuring soloist(s)	Ritornellos and Solo Sections in various closely related keys until the music returns to the tonic key and the movement ends)

FORMAL MODEL 7.1   Ritornello Form.

In ritornello forms, the larger ensemble is typically referred to as the **ripieno**, and if there is a group of soloists, that group is called the **concertino**. Example 7.1 diagrams the parts of the form in the first movement of "Summer" from Vivaldi's *Four Seasons*.

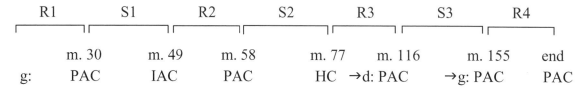

R1	S1	R2	S2	R3	S3	R4
	m. 30	m. 49	m. 58	m. 77 m. 116	m. 155	end
g:	PAC	IAC	PAC	HC →d: PAC	→g: PAC	PAC

Note: R1, R2, etc. are abbreviations for 1st Ritornello, 2nd Ritornello, etc. and S1, S2, etc. are abbreviations for 1st Solo Section, 2nd Solo Section, etc.

EXAMPLE 7.1   Diagram of Vivaldi, *Four Seasons*, "Summer," I.

Compare this diagram to the music (see Anthology, pp. 376–388). Note that the beginning of a ritornello is signaled by the return of the full ensemble presenting thematic material, not necessarily the return of the first theme. For example, while R2 and R3 end with material from R1, R4 does not include material from R1 at all.

One should also note the character of the solo sections; they are developmental and less tonally stable than the ritornello. For example, while no keys are tonicized in R1 or R2, the keys of B♭ and F are tonicized in S1. While there is a modulation in R3 to D minor, that modulation happens fairly quickly and then R3 is completely in D minor from m. 90 on. In fact, that modulation coupled with the dramatic shift in dynamics at m. 90 justifies an alternate interpretation that doesn't take the beginning of R3 until m. 90. A third factor that supports this alternate interpretation is that the basso continuo does not return until m. 90.

Nevertheless, the interpretation given as Example 7.1 still seems viable because the first violin section joins the solo violin at m. 77, so the solo violin line ceases to really be a solo at that point. However, one interpretation that really doesn't work is to take the beginning of R3 at m. 71 because the upper strings return at that point. Yes, they return, but only for a measure, and clearly in an accompanimental role (this is made clear by the fact that they drop out immediately after, and the solo violin continues unaccompanied for the next six measures). It is normal for composers to have some of the members from the ripieno accompany parts of the solo sections, though it sometimes can cloud the issue of what constitutes a ritornello when they do so.

In-Class Activity 7.1

Listen to the first movement of "Summer" from Vivaldi's *Four Seasons* and mark its phrase structure directly on the score (see Anthology, pp. 376–388). Compare your answers with other students in class.

Homework Assignment 7.1

Listen to the first movement of "Winter" from Vivaldi's *Four Seasons* and mark its phrase structure directly on the score (see Anthology, pp. 389–398). Then look at the incomplete phrase diagram of it in Homework Assignment 7.1 of your workbook; this diagram may or may not reflect your interpretation. Fill in the blanks with formal labels (i.e. ritornellos and solo sections), cadence types, sequence types, measure numbers or key areas, as appropriate (blanks before colons are for keys).

Types of Concertos and Concerto Movements

The **concerto grosso** was a type of concerto popular in the Baroque period that pits a small group of soloists against a larger ensemble. While solo concertos were also common in the early Baroque, they became much more popular in the late Baroque, and almost entirely displaced the concerto grosso in the Classical and Romantic periods. However, the prevalence of ritornello form in the first and last movements of three-movement Baroque concertos is common to both solo concertos and concerti grossi. The middle movements are in a wide variety of forms: binaries, ternaries, composite ternaries, fugues, and continuous variations are all possibilities.

Most concertos are in three movements with a fast-slow-fast tempo scheme; this tradition was established by Vivaldi and Bach (Bach as a young man studied Vivaldi's concertos, and his own concertos, like Vivaldi's, are typically in three movements). However, other Baroque composers such as Corelli and Handel would often write concertos with between four and six movements. Ritornello form would often be used in these concertos, but could be found in any movement; first and last movements were just as likely to be binaries, ternaries, composite ternaries, fugues, or continuous variations. Nevertheless, after the Baroque period the three-movement concerto model became firmly established, and one finds far fewer concertos that depart from it.

In-Class Activity 7.2

Listen to the first movement of Bach's Brandenburg Concerto No. 1 and mark the beginning of each ritornello and each solo section directly on the score (see Anthology, pp. 24–33). Then listen again and mark its phrase structure directly on the score. Compare your answers with other students in the class.

Imitation in Baroque Concerto Movements

In many Baroque concerto movements the prevailing texture is imitative, and in some cases the parts of a fugue are clearly distinguishable. In such cases, the best understanding might be one that combines the models for fugue and ritornello form, in much the same way that Chapter 5 explains "When I am Laid in Earth" as a combination of a continuous variation form and a simple binary form (see p. 65). The different parts of the two forms are independent of one another: sometimes the alternations between ritornello and solo section will coincide with the alternations between episode and restatement, but many times they will not. Example 7.2 diagrams the parts of each form in the third movement of Bach's Brandenburg Concerto No. 2.

Exposition	Epis.	Restat.	Epis.	Restat.		Epis.	Restat.	Epis.	
(tr. ob. vl. fl.) 33	41(tr.)	47	57	(vl. ob. rip.) 79			107(ob. fl. rip.)124		end
S1		R1	S2	R2	S3	R3	S4	R4	
		47	57	72	85	97	107	119	end

EXAMPLE 7.2   Diagram of Bach, Brandenburg Concerto No. 2, III.

Listen to this movement without the score while following the diagram (watch your instructor cue the different themes as they enter). Unlike the beginning of a conventional fugue, the subject here is not presented alone but is instead accompanied by a countersubject from the very start. And unlike the beginning of a conventional ritornello form, this movement does not begin with a ritornello, but rather with a solo section. Nevertheless, the alternations between ritornellos and solo sections are very audible, as are the alternations between episodes and restatements. When the alternations in the two different forms coincide, they help to reinforce one another and serve to create a stronger formal marker: two such locations are m. 47 (the beginning of the second episode and the beginning of the first ritornello) and m. 57 (the ending of that episode and the ending of the first ritornello). The last movements of the fourth and fifth Brandenburg Concertos also combine fugal form with ritornello form, though each one adopts its own unique way of combining the two (i.e. the specifics of how episodes and restatements are aligned with solo sections and restatements vary from movement to movement).

Classical Concerto Form

When musicians talk about "concerto form" they are typically referring not to ritornello form, but to a kind of concerto form that developed in the Classical period. **Classical concerto form** is a blending of sonata form and ritornello form that typically features an extended unaccompanied solo called a **cadenza** either just before the closing section or in the middle of it. It is commonly found in first movements of Classical-period concertos, and the form is sometimes seen in Romantic-period concertos as well.

	Orch. Exposition	Solo Exposition	Development	Recapitulation
	P B (S) C	P B S C	(motivic dev.)	P B S C (w/cadenza)
maj.:	I--------------------I	→V	(unstable)	I---------------------------I
min.:	i--------------------i	→III or v		i---------------------------i

Orch.= Orchestral, P = Primary Theme, B = Bridge, S = Secondary Theme, C = Closing (Roman numerals indicate key areas)

FORMAL MODEL 7.2 Classical Concerto Form.

There are two different expositions in Classical concerto form: one that features the orchestra followed by another that features the soloist. The two expositions in a Classical concerto form are often referred to as a **double exposition**. During the orchestral exposition, the soloist either plays an accompanimental role or doesn't play at all, the second theme does not always appear (this is why the model has it in parentheses), and the orchestra presents all of its thematic material in the tonic key. It is not until the solo exposition that we hear the characteristic modulation to the secondary key area that helps to define sonata form.

Note the differences between the model for Classical concerto form and the model for sonata form that you studied earlier: 1) there are no repeat signs; 2) while the exposition is not literally repeated, the material is heard twice, though in two different versions; 3) the modulation to the secondary key in the exposition does not happen until the solo exposition; and 4) one expects to hear a cadenza somewhere in the closing section, or immediately after it (in which case, a coda will follow). The first movement of Mozart's Piano Concerto in D major, K. 107 is a good example of Classical concerto form:

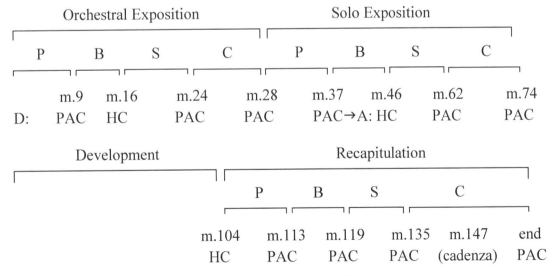

EXAMPLE 7.3 Diagram of Mozart, Piano Concerto in D major, K. 107, I.

Compare this diagram to the music (see Anthology, pp. 335–343). Just as was true for sonata forms, in Classical concerto forms it is often difficult to determine exactly where one part of the exposition or recapitulation ends and the next part begins: sometimes it is hard to pinpoint the ending of the primary theme and beginning of the bridge, or the ending of the bridge and beginning of the secondary theme, or the ending of the secondary theme and beginning of the closing. It is very rare, however, that all three of these are difficult to find. In the first movement of Mozart's Piano Concerto in D Major, K. 107, it is particularly difficult to determine the end of the second theme and beginning of the closing in the solo exposition and recapitulation. Example 7.3 reflects one interpretation, but there are two other viable choices: one could take the beginning of the closing as early as m. 54 (which, if one is to be logically consistent, would require taking it at m. 127 in the recapitulation), or one could take the beginning of the closing as late as m. 70 (which, if one is to be logically consistent, would require taking it at m. 148 in the recapitulation).

The ambiguity regarding where to take the end of the second theme and the beginning of the closing was created by Mozart through the addition of material to the solo exposition that was not present in the orchestral exposition. It is unclear whether that material serves to expand the end of the second theme or the beginning of the closing, or whether it serves neither but functions more independently. This last possibility should be considered another interpretation, one in which the solo exposition and recapitulation each have *five* parts, the usual four plus the added music in mm. 54–69 and mm. 127–147, respectively. This might remind you of the exposition from the first movement of Beethoven's Symphony No. 3, in which there were clearly more than four parts. Nevertheless, it is at least possible in the first movement of Mozart's K. 107 to consider the added music as expanding one of the four parts from the model, though such an interpretation is no better or worse than one that interprets the added music as being independent of those parts.

The model given for Classical concerto form (Formal Model 7.2) does not show alternations between the full ensemble and the soloist as the model for ritornello form did because there is such a wide variety of ways in which these alternations can be aligned with the elements of sonata form discussed above. However, there are certainly some generalizations that can be made. First, the orchestral exposition is in effect like a large ritornello, and the solo exposition begins with a solo section. Second, the closing of the solo exposition and the recapitulation often feature the full ensemble, since louder dynamics and fuller textures define the character of a closing. Third, the development will primarily feature the soloist, though one or more ritornellos may also occur. Fourth, an alternation between the full ensemble and soloist will mark the beginning of the recapitulation, with either the soloist yielding to the full ensemble at that point, or vice versa. Finally, the cadenza will be preceded and followed by ritornellos, and the movement will always end with a ritornello.

Homework Assignment 7.2

Listen to the first movement of Mozart's Piano Concerto in D major, K. 107 and mark its phrase structure directly on the score (see Anthology, pp. 335–343). Then look at the incomplete phrase diagram of it in Homework Assignment 7.2 of your workbook; this diagram may or may not reflect your interpretation. Fill in the blanks with formal labels (i.e. ritornellos and solo sections), cadence types, sequence types, measure numbers or key areas, as appropriate (blanks before colons are for keys).

The Cadenza

The **cadenza** of a concerto is an unaccompanied solo for the featured instrument that is often inserted near the end of movements in Classical concerto form. Cadenzas have historically been improvised, and so the music of the cadenza often does not appear in the full score, though few soloists actually improvise their cadenzas today. The approach and the conclusion of a cadenza were codified in the Classical period. The cadenza would be preceded by the full ensemble reaching and then holding a cadential $^6_4$ chord. The perfect authentic cadence expected by the audience at that point would then be "interrupted" as the orchestra stops playing and the soloist begins playing unaccompanied. The soloist would then proceed to improvise a cadenza (or to play a memorized cadenza) based on thematic material from the exposition. The cadenza would end on what is commonly referred to as the **pre-tutti trill**: the soloist would perform a trill on scale-degree 2 and this would be the signal for the conductor to prepare the orchestra to start playing again. The trill on scale-degree 2 would substitute for the dominant chord (except for piano concertos, in which the dominant chord would often be played with the trill), and the orchestra would come back in on the tonic chord, thus finally completing the perfect authentic cadence that was "interrupted" by the cadenza.

Example 7.4 illustrates with a reduction how these conventions are realized in the first movement of Mozart's Piano Concerto in D Major, K.107, as well as how the cadenza in a Classical concerto interrupts a perfect authentic cadence.

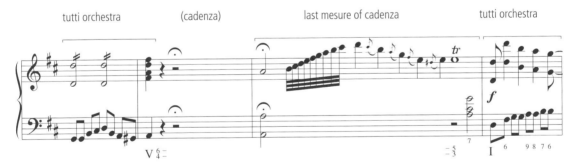

EXAMPLE 7.4   Music preceding and following the cadenza in K107, I.

Compare the example to the full score (see Anthology, p. 343).

In-Class Activity 7.3

Look at and listen to the preparations and resolutions of the cadenzas in the first movements of Mozart's Piano Concerto in E♭ major, K. 271 (see Anthology, p. 371) and Brahms' Violin Concerto in D major (see Anthology, p. 216). Do both of these examples follow the usual formula? If not, what is different?

Homework Assignment 7.3

The first movement of Mozart's Piano Concerto in E♭ major, K. 271 is an expansion of the Classical concerto model in that it has multiple bridges and closings. Listen to the movement and mark the formal structure (i.e. the orchestral exposition, primary theme, bridge, etc.) directly on the score (see Anthology, pp. 344–372). Then look at the incomplete formal diagram of it in Homework Assignment 7.3 of your workbook; this diagram may or may not reflect your interpretation. Fill in the blanks with P (primary theme), B1 (1st bridge), B2 (2nd bridge), B3 (3rd bridge), S (secondary theme), C1 (first closing), or C2 (second closing) by comparing the material after m. 62 to the same material in the orchestral exposition. Finally, answer the questions that follow the diagram.

Concertos in the Romantic Period

It is hard to generalize about the forms of movements from Romantic period concertos, but some observations about them are worth noting. First, the model of Classical concerto form given as Formal Model 7.2 can still be used to understand a number of concertos from the Romantic period, especially those written by composers typically considered conservative relative to the overall spirit of the times (e.g. Brahms). Second, the alternation of tutti sections and solo sections, fundamental to concertos since the beginning of the genre, is still important to many Romantic concertos. Third, even though many Romantic concertos do not follow the model for Classical concerto form, sonata form still seems to be an important shaping force. Many are still based on the model for sonata form, but the double exposition of the Classical concerto is replaced by a single exposition in which the alternation between tutti and solo presentations is incorporated (e.g. the piano concertos by Grieg, Schumann, and Rachmaninoff). Fourth, the key relationships in Romantic concertos, just like those in sonata forms, are often less predictable than their Classical counterparts.

The first movement of Brahms' Violin Concerto in D Major is a good example of a relatively conservative approach to concerto form in the Romantic period. Example 7.5 (opposite) provides a formal diagram of the movement.

Compare this diagram to the music (see Anthology, pp. 185–218). The double exposition from the Classical concerto form model is maintained, utilizing the optional omission of the secondary theme in the orchestral exposition, so that the soloist is the first to present that theme. The alternation of soloist and tutti ensemble is familiar and the ordering of thematic materials is also what one would expect.

However, Brahms' sense of Romanticism is felt in this movement's key areas. First, modal mixture is important to the relationship of the themes in each exposition and in the recapitulation as well because the change of mode from major to parallel minor marks the dramatic beginning of the closing theme each time it occurs. Second, two chromatic mediant relationships are featured in the recapitulation. The second theme in the recapitulation is first presented in F♯ major, before it gives way to the expected primary key of D major, and before the recapitulation is over, the beginning of the primary theme

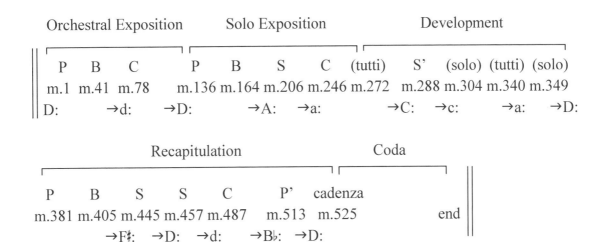

EXAMPLE 7.5   Formal Diagram of Brahms, Violin Concerto in D Major, I.

reappears unexpectedly in B♭ major before the full ensemble quickly steers the music back to D major in preparation for the cadenza.

In-Class Activity 7.4

Listen to the first movement of Brahms' Violin Concerto in D Major with the score and mark the phrase structure in the solo exposition (see Anthology, pp. 185–218). Compare your answers with others in the class.

In More Detail: Metrical Dissonance

Hemiolas, rhythms that create a feeling of two beats against three beats, or vice versa (see p. 00), are one of the most common forms of metrical dissonances, but other kinds of metrical dissonances are also possible. Brahms in particular loved to explore other possibilities, and in his Violin Concerto, one can hear an example of five beats set against three:

EXAMPLE 7.6   Brahms, Violin Concerto, I, mm. 53–60.

The counterpoint between the outer voices in mm. 53–57 repeats twice, and because it is five quarter notes long, it sounds as though it is in 5/4. However, probably because 5/4 is an asymmetrical meter and because at this point in the movement we've heard fifty-two measures of music in 3/4, we still hear 3/4 competing against 5/4 in this passage.

There are two kinds of metrical dissonances: *grouping dissonances* and *displacement dissonances*. **Grouping dissonances** are metrical dissonances in which there is a conflict between at least two different meters (one of these is almost always the notated meter), as in hemiolas or in passages such as the one given as Example 7.6. **Displacement dissonances** are metrical dissonances in which there is a conflict between at least two different beats that could be interpreted as downbeats (one of these is almost always the notated downbeat). Brahms was also interested in displacement dissonances, and in the fourth movement of his Fourth Symphony, one can hear an example of beat 2 temporarily being set up to sound like beat 1.

EXAMPLE 7.7   Brahms, Fourth Symphony, IV, mm. 16–26.

Because the bass notes in this passage consistently come on what is notated as beat 2, and because all of the melodic entrances are also on beat 2, beat 2 actually sounds like beat 1 (the harmony changes on beat 2 actually start back in m. 9). There is a jarring effect when the notated downbeat suddenly becomes the sounding downbeat again at m. 24. Listen to Example 7.7 and conduct the *sounding* meter: this will require you to start conducting with a three pattern on what is notated as beat 2 in m. 16, then conduct a two pattern at the end of m. 24 (see above) in order to realign your pattern with the notated meter in m. 25 when it becomes the sounding meter again.

Notice that, while there is a strong conflict between the notated meter and the sounding meter in this passage, both meters are 3/4, and so it is not a grouping dissonance. Grouping dissonances, if they go on for any length of time, will go in and out of phase as the downbeats of the conflicting meters periodically align (e.g. in Example 7.6 we can see that the downbeats in 5/4 and 3/4 align after five measures). The downbeats in displacement dissonances will never align, no matter how long the dissonance lasts.

Grieg's Piano Concerto in A Minor provides a good example of another common approach to writing the first movement of a concerto in the Romantic period: the double exposition is replaced by a single exposition in which the primary and secondary themes are presented by some combination of tutti and solo statements. A formal diagram of the movement is given as Example 7.8.

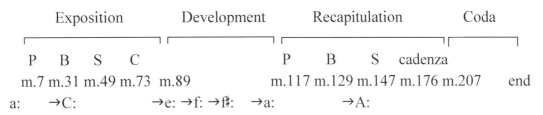

EXAMPLE 7.8   Formal Diagram of Grieg, Piano Concerto in A Minor, I.

Listen to this movement without the score while following the diagram (watch your instructor cue the different themes as they enter). Notice how the double exposition of Classical concerto form is replaced by a single exposition in which the primary and secondary themes are presented by some combination of tutti and solo statements. In m. 7 (after a brief introduction by the soloist), the primary theme is played by the tutti ensemble and then immediately passed to the soloist, who plays a varied repetition of it. In m. 49, the first two phrases of the secondary theme are presented by the tutti ensemble and those are immediately echoed by the soloist in a varied repetition, then the soloist presents the rest of the theme (this same pattern of presentation is used when the secondary theme comes back in m. 147). In m. 117 (the beginning of the recapitulation), the first three phrases of the primary theme are played by the soloist and then the last phrase is played by the tutti ensemble.

There are two other ways in which this movement defies the expectations established by Classical concertos. First, the closing material from the exposition never comes back in the recapitulation. Second, the preparation and the resolution of the cadenza are both different from what one would expect in a Classical concerto. Instead of using a cadential $^6_4$ chord to prepare the cadenza, Grieg uses the VI chord, having the orchestra drop out after a huge deceptive cadence. And while there is a pre-tutti trill on scale-degree 2 at the very end of the cadenza, it does not resolve to scale-degree 1 supported by tonic harmony, but instead it resolves to scale-degree 5 supported by V$^4_3$/iv.

Homework Assignment 7.4

The first movement of Mozart's Clarinet Concerto in A major, K. 622 is an expansion of the Classical concerto model in that it has multiple bridge and closing sections. Listen to the movement and mark the formal structure (i.e. the orchestral exposition, primary theme, bridge, etc.) directly on the score. Then look at the incomplete formal diagram of it in Homework Assignment 7.4 of your workbook; this diagram may or may not reflect your interpretation. Fill in the blanks with P (primary theme), B1 (1st bridge), B2 (2nd bridge),

S (secondary theme), C1 (first closing), C2 (second closing), and C3 (third closing) by comparing the material after m. 56 to the same material in the orchestral exposition. Then answer the questions that follow the diagram.

Homework Assignment 7.5

Listen to the first movement of Mozart's Flute Concerto in G major, K. 313 and mark its phrase structure directly on the score. Then look at the incomplete phrase diagram in Homework Assignment 7.5 of your workbook; this diagram may or may not reflect your interpretation. Fill in the blanks with formal labels (i.e. exposition, primary theme, bridge, etc.), cadence types, sequence types, measure numbers or key areas, as appropriate (blanks before colons are for keys). Finally, answer the questions that follow the diagram. Note that this diagram does not include the cadenza.

Homework Assignment 7.6

Listen to the first movement of Mendelssohn's Violin Concerto, Op. 64 and mark its phrase structure directly on the score. Then look at the incomplete phrase diagram in Homework Assignment 7.6 of your workbook; this diagram may or may not reflect your interpretation. Fill in the blanks with formal labels (i.e. exposition, primary theme, bridge, etc.), cadence types, sequence types, measure numbers or key areas, as appropriate (blanks before colons are for keys). Finally, answer the questions that follow the diagram. Note that this diagram does not include the cadenza.

Homework Assignment 7.7

Listen to the first movement of Haydn's Trumpet Concerto in E♭ Major and mark its phrase structure directly on the score. Then look at the incomplete phrase diagram in Homework Assignment 7.7 of your workbook; this diagram may or may not reflect your interpretation. Fill in the blanks with formal labels (i.e. exposition, primary theme, bridge, etc.), cadence types, sequence types, measure numbers or key areas, as appropriate (blanks before colons are for keys). Finally, answer the questions on the back of the page. Note that this diagram does not include the cadenza.

Homework Assignment 7.8

Choose a movement from a Romantic period concerto that is in sonata form or classical concerto form and that is not included in the Anthology. Then write a one-page essay summarizing its form and how it differs from the classical concerto model (see page 83).

Chapter Review

1   A **ritornello** is a passage featuring the whole ensemble, and a regular alternation between ritornellos and solo sections throughout an entire movement is called **ritornello form**. Movements in ritornello form are common in the first and last movements of Baroque concertos. The ritornellos are passages that feature the larger ensemble, while the solo sections feature the soloist(s). While a ritornello usually presents thematic material, a **solo section** often develops motives from the ritornellos.

2   In ritornello forms, the larger ensemble is typically referred to as the **ripieno**, and if there is a group of soloists, that group is called the **concertino**.

3   The **concerto grosso** was a type of concerto popular in the Baroque period that pits a small group of soloists against a larger ensemble. While popular in the Baroque, the solo concerto also became popular in the late Baroque period, and almost entirely displaced the concerto grosso in the Classical and Romantic periods. However, the prevalence of ritornello form in the first and last movements of Baroque concertos was common to both solo concertos and concerti grossi.

4   **Classical concerto form** is a blending of sonata form and ritornello form that typically features an extended unaccompanied solo called a **cadenza** either just before the final ritornello or in the middle of it. It was commonly used in first movements of Classical-period concertos, and was sometimes used in Romantic-period concertos as well.

5   There are two different expositions in Classical concerto form, one that features the orchestra followed by another that features the soloist. The two expositions in a Classical concerto form are often referred to as a **double exposition**. During the orchestral exposition, the soloist either plays an accompanimental role, or doesn't play at all, the second theme does not always appear (this is why the model has it in parentheses), and the orchestra presents all of its thematic material in the tonic key. It is not until the solo exposition that we hear the characteristic modulation to the secondary key area that helps to define sonata form.

6   The **cadenza** of a concerto is an unaccompanied solo for the featured instrument that is often inserted near the end of movements in Classical concerto form. Cadenzas have historically been improvised, and so the music of the cadenza often does not appear in the full score, though few soloists actually improvise their cadenzas today.

7   The approach and the conclusion of a cadenza were codified in the Classical period. The cadenza would be preceded by the full ensemble reaching and then holding a cadential $^6_4$ chord. The soloist would then proceed to improvise a cadenza based on all of the thematic material from the exposition. The cadenza would end on what is commonly referred to as the **pre-tutti trill**: the soloist would perform a trill on scale-degree 2 and this would be the signal for the conductor to prepare the orchestra to start playing again.

chapter 8

Rondo Forms

Rondo forms are defined by the regular alternation of an A section with other sections. They are similar to ternary forms in that the A section is tonally closed and it returns at the end; however, while a ternary form has just one contrasting section, rondos have two or more such sections.

Five-Part Rondos

Five-part rondos have three distinct sections, labeled A, B, and C, which are presented in the following order:

A	B	A	C	A

FORMAL MODEL 8.1   Five-Part Rondo Form.

The A sections in rondos are often called **refrains**. These are almost always in the tonic key, while the other sections are often in contrasting keys. The last movement from Haydn's Piano Sonata in D Major Hob. XVI: 37 (see Anthology, pp. 236–238) is a good example of a five-part rondo.

Though sections in a rondo can be as short as just a couple of phrases, they can also be long enough to be in some kind of binary form, making the rondo itself a composite form (see Chapter 3). The longer refrains would often have abbreviated returns, though that is not

```
        A            B            A            C      trans.     A
  ‖: :‖‖: :‖‖:   :‖‖: :‖‖:   :‖‖: :‖‖:   :‖‖: :‖    ‖     ‖           ‖
mm.1-8, 9-20, 21-28, 29-40, 41-48, 49-60, 61-68, 69-80, 81-93, 94-109, 110-end
keys: D, A,  D ; d, F,     d ; D, A,    D ; G            ; D   ; D, A,      D
```

EXAMPLE 8.1   Formal Diagram of Haydn, Piano Sonata, Hob. XVI: 37, III.

the case in the Haydn example above. In the Haydn, all three sections are in rounded binary form; the A and B sections are continuous rounded binaries, while the C section is a sectional rounded binary. Note that while the repeat signs are missing from the final presentation of the A section, the repeat scheme is still present: mm. 102–109 are just a varied repetition of mm. 94–101, and mm. 122–133 are just a varied repetition of mm. 110–121.

In a rondo, one section might begin immediately after the previous section is over, or there might be a brief transition between sections. In the Haydn example above, such a passage connects the end of the C section with the return of the final A section (mm. 81–93). Because transitions between any two sections in a rondo may or may not occur, they are not included in the model for the five-part rondo given above.

In-Class Activity 8.1

Listen to the third movement of Haydn's Piano Sonata in D Major, Hob. XVI: 37 and mark its phrase structure directly on the score (see Anthology, pp. 236–238). Compare your answers with other students in class.

Rondos in More Than Five Parts

While rondos often have five parts and can be understood in terms of the five-part rondo model given above, they just as often have more than five parts and can only be understood as some kind of expansion of that model. What binds all rondos together is an adherence to the rondo principle: *primary thematic material is presented in alternation with multiple contrasting sections.* Sometimes more than two contrasting sections are used, sometimes one of the returns to the primary thematic material is omitted so that two contrasting sections are presented back to back, and sometimes a combination of these variants are found. Example 8.2 provides a sample of rondos in more than five parts to illustrate the variety that composers have found when expressing themselves through the rondo principle.

Bach, Partita No. 3 in E for Violin Solo, Gavotte:	A B A C A D A E A
Mozart, Piano Sonata, K. 331, Rondo alla Turca:	A B C B A B Coda
Haydn, Trio in G Major, Hob. XV: 25, Finale:	A B C A D A
Beethoven, Violin Sonata No. 4, Op. 23, Finale:	A B A C A B C A
Schubert, Piano Sonata, Op. 42, IV:	A B A C A D A B A' C' Coda
Schumann, Novelletten, Op. 21, No. 7:	A B C A D A C A

EXAMPLE 8.2   Some Rondos in More Than Five Parts.

Among the rondos listed above, all but the Mozart and Beethoven have more than two contrasting sections. Note that in the rondo from Mozart's Sonata, K. 331, the B section actually returns more than the A section, and so in some sense the B section takes on the A section's usual function. Also note that in the Haydn, Beethoven, and Schumann rondos listed above, one of the returns to the primary thematic material is omitted.

Sonata-Rondos

As the name suggests, **sonata-rondos** are forms that combine elements of the rondo with elements of sonata form. The model for a sonata-rondo is given below:

	Exposition (= A B A)				Development* (=C)	Recapitulation (= A B A)				
	P	(Br)	S	(Cl)	P		P	(Br)	S	(Cl)	P
maj.: I			→V		I		I---------------------------------I
min.: i			→III or v		i		i---------------------------------i

P = Primary Theme, Br = Bridge, S = Secondary Theme, Cl = Closing (Roman numerals indicate key areas)

* The development could be replaced by new contrasting thematic material.

FORMAL MODEL 8.2 Sonata-Rondo Form.

In the sonata-rondo, the primary theme of the sonata form also assumes the role of the refrain in a rondo. The brackets and parenthetical commentary at the top of the model show how the sonata-rondo can be thought of as a seven-part rondo with the first three parts grouped together to form an exposition, and the last three parts grouped together to form a recapitulation. The music that occupies the fourth position of the rondo structure might develop material from the exposition, in which case it would sound like the development in a sonata form. However, it might instead present new thematic material and thus sound more like a contrasting C section in a rondo (see asterisk in model), in which case the label "Development" doesn't really seem appropriate. It's even possible for a composer to do a little of both, as Beethoven does in the third movement of his Piano Sonata, Op. 13 (to be discussed in more detail below).

The lower parts of the sonata-rondo model show how it can be thought of as a sonata form with the first theme returning at the end of both the exposition and the recapitulation as a refrain would in a rondo. The "Br" and "Cl" representing "bridge" and "closing," respectively, are placed in parentheses because one or both may be omitted in favor of a more rondo-like presentation. What really defines the sonata-rondo form as more than just a seven-part rondo is not the presence of a bridge, a closing or a development, but the introduction of secondary thematic material in the key of the dominant or mediant and its subsequent transposition to the tonic in a recapitulation. Examples 8.3 illustrates how the third movement from Beethoven's Piano Sonata, Op. 13 (see Anthology, pp. 38–43) is an example of sonata-rondo form:

	Exposition					C section		Recapitulation				Coda
	P	Br	S	Cl	P		trans.	P	S	Cl	P	
m.1		18	25	37	62	79	107	121	134	143	171	182	end
c:		→	E♭:		→c:	; A♭:	→c:	C:			c:	

EXAMPLE 8.3 Formal Diagram of Beethoven's Piano Sonata, Op. 13, III.

In this particular sonata-rondo, there is a C section rather than a development, though the transition that sits on a dominant bass pedal sounds very much like it could be the conclusion of a development section. The C section is defined clearly by having its own stable key—A♭ major—as well as its own stable form, a continuous variations based on a descending fifths sequence. Note that the bridge does not return in the recapitulation. However, the telltale key scheme of sonata form is present here—a return to the primary tonic accompanies the return of the secondary theme (though the mode is major rather than minor)—and that is enough to define it as a sonata-rondo.

In-Class Activity 8.2

Listen to the third movement of Beethoven's Piano Sonata, Op. 13 and mark its phrase structure directly on the score (see Anthology, pp. 38–43). Then compare your answers with other students in class.

The fourth movement of Beethoven's Symphony No. 2 (see Anthology, pp. 44–63) is also an example of sonata-rondo form:

Exposition					Development		Recapitulation					Coda	
P	Br	S	Cl	P			P	Br	S	Cl	P		
m.1	26	52	84	108	119	155	185	210	236	268	292, 299		end
D:		→A:		→D:	d:	→f♯:	; D:						

EXAMPLE 8.4   Formal Diagram of Beethoven's Symphony No. 2, IV.

Unlike the third movement of Beethoven's Piano Sonata, Op. 13, this sonata-rondo has a development as well as all four parts of the recapitulation. While this symphony is from Beethoven's early period, the coda is nevertheless Romantic in its proportions—it's actually longer than the entire recapitulation.

Homework Assignment 8.1

Listen to the fourth movement of Mozart's Symphony No. 35, and mark its phrase structure directly on the score (see Anthology, pp. 300–314). Then look at the incomplete phrase diagram of it in Homework Assignment 8.1 of your workbook; this diagram may or may not reflect your interpretation. Fill in the blanks with formal labels (i.e. exposition, primary theme, etc.), cadence types, sequence types, measure numbers or key areas, as appropriate (blanks before colons are for keys).

In-Class Activity 8.3

Listen to the fourth movement of Beethoven's Symphony No. 2 and mark its phrase structure directly on the score (see Anthology, pp. 44–63). Then compare your answers with other students in class.

Homework Assignment 8.2

Listen to the third movement of Mozart's Piano Sonata, K. 333 and mark its phrase structure directly on the score (see Anthology, pp. 282–287). Then look at the incomplete phrase diagram of it in Homework Assignment 8.2 of your workbook; this diagram may or may not reflect your interpretation. Fill in the blanks with formal labels (i.e. exposition, primary theme, etc.), cadence types, sequence types, measure numbers or key areas, as appropriate (blanks before colons are for keys). Then answer the five questions that follow the diagram.

Historical Trends in the Rondo

The origins of the rondo go all the way back to the Medieval period, though this text only focuses on its use in the common-practice period (1600–1900). In the Baroque period and in earlier periods, the refrain (A section) of a rondo was often just two phrases long; during that time it was also common to write rondos as independent pieces, though they were also used as movements in multi-movement works. In the Classical period it became more common for the refrain of a rondo to be longer and in some kind of binary form, and the other sections were often longer as well. After the Baroque period, it became much less common for rondos to be written as independent pieces, but Classical and Romantic composers often chose to write rondos or sonata-rondos for the last movements of their sonatas, symphonies, concertos, and chamber works.

Concerto-Rondos

Most Classical and many Romantic concertos end with a movement in rondo or sonata-rondo form. However, Mozart created a third kind of rondo form for the finales of his later concertos (Beethoven's Fifth Piano Concerto uses this form as well). This third form, often called **concerto-rondo form**, combines sonata form with rondo form, but unlike the sonata-rondo form, the material of the refrain is different than the material that serves as the primary theme of the sonata form and stands outside of the exposition and recapitulation:

```
        Rfr          Exposition        Rfr  Development* (Rfr)   Recapitulation      Rfr
       ┌──┐      ┌──────────────┐     ┌──┐ ┌──────────┐┌──┐    ┌─────────────┐    ┌──┐
               P    (Br)  S   Cl                           (P) (Br)  S   Cl
 maj.: I               →V             I                   I-----------------------------------I
 min.: i               →III or v      i                   i-----------------------------------i
```

Rfr = Refrain, P = Primary Theme, Br = Bridge, S = Secondary Theme, Cl = Closing
* The development could be replaced by new contrasting thematic material.
FORMAL MODEL 8.3 Concerto-Rondo Form.

As with the sonata-rondo, the fourth part of the concerto-rondo can serve as a development section, it can present a new contrasting theme, or it can do both. Those parts of the model in parentheses above are sometimes omitted, but their omissions are not enough to mask the form's relationship to the rondo or to the sonata form. The main thematic material in the first two refrains of a concerto-rondo is typically begun by the soloist and concluded by the orchestra. When the third refrain is present, its main thematic material is presented by either the soloist or the orchestra but generally not by both. The main thematic material in the final refrain is typically begun by the orchestra and concluded by the soloist (after the thematic material is concluded, the orchestra then joins the soloist to end the movement).

The third movement of Mozart's Piano Concerto in D minor, K. 466 (no score provided) is a good example of concerto-rondo form. Listen and use Example 8.5 to follow along while your instructor cues the different parts of the form.

```
        Rfr     Exposition       Rfr   Development   Recapitulation     Rfr    Coda
       ┌──┐   ┌──────────┐     ┌──┐  ┌───────────┐ ┌──────────┐     ┌──┐  ┌────────┐
             P   Br  S   Cl                (P)       P   Br   S   Cl         (Cl)
 m. 1   63  92 110 139 167   180 (196)    230 271 289 302  346   354       end
 d:          →F:        d:           →a:       →g: →d:
```

EXAMPLE 8.5   Formal Diagram of Mozart, Piano Concerto, K. 466, III.

The third refrain is omitted in this example, and the beginning of the recapitulation is in G minor, though it moves quickly enough to the primary key. To further complicate matters, the refrain theme is added to the end of the primary theme in the exposition (mm. 73–79, this addition to the primary theme is not found in the recapitulation). Despite these deviations from the concerto-rondo model, one can hear the presence of both sonata form principles and rondo form principles clearly articulated in this movement, and interacting in a way that is more reflective of the concerto-rondo model than of the model for sonata-rondo.

In More Detail: Model-Defying Forms

For the most part, the examples in this book are of music that clearly fit one formal model or another, with relatively few examples from the repertoire that, while clearly derived from a model, nevertheless challenge it in some important way. This might leave one with the false impression that the goal of formal analysis is to identify the models, when in fact it is far more important to understand how the music analyzed relates to the models, and in places where it is different, to understand that difference and its consequences for performance.

A good example of a model-defying form can be found in the fourth movement of Haydn's Symphony No. 101 (see Anthology, pp. 239–257). A formal diagram of the movement is given as Example 8.6.

Exposition (= A B A)					Development (=C)		Recap.-like Coda (= A)	
P	Br	S	Cl	P		fugato	P'(only first two phrases)	
m. 1	28	62	75	103	138	189	233	end
D:	→A:		→D:		d:	D:		

EXAMPLE 8.6 Formal Diagram of Haydn, Symphony No. 101, IV.

It proceeds as a sonata-rondo form would up until about m.198, but then fails to deliver the recapitulation that one would expect in a sonata-rondo. Instead it enters into what sounds a lot like a coda. The secondary theme does not return in the key of the tonic (it actually does not return at all), and this has been identified as crucial to the definition of the sonata-rondo. Because of this, one might decide that the label of five-part rondo is more appropriate, since there are two clearly contrasting sections, and the A section returns twice as well, creating an ABACA design. However, this understanding ignores the character of those contrasting sections: mm. 60–75 sound like a second theme because it is approached like a second theme—on a sustained dominant pedal—and because it is followed by what sounds like closing material—the entrance at m. 75 is a dramatic shift from a thin-textured soft dynamic to a full-textured loud dynamic. The music in mm. 138–231 sounds very much like a development section because it begins with a dramatic shift from a thin-textured soft dynamic to a full-textured loud dynamic, it contains a lot of motivic repetition and sequences, and it ends with a fugato. Ultimately, whether one calls this a sonata-rondo or a five-part rondo is immaterial: what matters is that one recognizes those elements that relate to sonata forms and those that relate to rondo forms, and recognizes how those have been combined in a different way here.

Homework Assignment 8.3

Listen to the fourth movement of Haydn's Symphony No. 101 and mark its phrase structure directly on the score (see Anthology, pp. 239–257). Then look at the incomplete phrase diagram of it in Homework Assignment 8.3 of your workbook; this diagram may or may not reflect your interpretation. Fill in the blanks with formal labels (i.e. exposition, primary theme, etc.), cadence types, sequence types, measure numbers or key areas, as appropriate (blanks before colons are for keys). Then answer the question that follows the diagram.

Homework Assignment 8.4

Listen to the second movement of Beethoven's Piano Sonata, Op. 13 and mark its phrase structure directly on the score. Then look at the incomplete phrase diagram of it in Homework Assignment 8.4 of your workbook; this diagram may or may not reflect your interpretation. Fill in the blanks with formal labels (A, B, C, etc.), cadence types, measure numbers or key areas, as appropriate. Then answer the questions that follow the diagram.

Homework Assignment 8.5

Listen to the second movement of Mozart's *Eine kleine Nachtmusik* and mark its phrase structure directly on the score (see Anthology, pp. 288–299). Then look at the incomplete phrase diagram of it in Homework Assignment 8.5 of your workbook; this diagram may or may not reflect your interpretation. Fill in the blanks with formal labels (A, B, C, etc.), cadence types, measure numbers or key areas, as appropriate. Then answer the questions that follow the diagram.

Homework Assignment 8.6

Listen to the fourth movement of Mozart's *Eine kleine Nachtmusik* and mark its phrase structure directly on the score (see Anthology, pp. 288–299). Then look at the incomplete phrase diagram of it in Homework Assignment 8.6 of your workbook; this diagram may or may not reflect your interpretation. Fill in the blanks with formal labels (A, B, C, etc.), cadence types, measure numbers or key areas, as appropriate. Then answer the questions that follow the diagram.

Homework Assignment 8.7

Choose a rondo from the Romantic period that is not included in the Anthology. Analyze its form, phrase structure, key areas, and harmonic sequences by preparing an annotated score. To show its phrase structure, mark each phrase ending where it occurs with the cadence type below the system and each subphrase ending with a comma above the system. Also, label key areas and harmonic sequences (by type) where they occur.

Homework Assignment 8.8

Choose a rondo movement from the Baroque period that is not included in the Anthology. Analyze its form, phrase structure, key areas, and harmonic sequences by preparing an annotated score. To show its phrase structure, mark each phrase ending where it occurs with the cadence type below the system and each subphrase ending with a comma above the system. Also, label key areas and harmonic sequences (by type) where they occur.

Homework Assignment 8.9

Find a poem that has a rondo-like structure and then write a 1–2 page essay that describes how the poem could be set musically. Consider text painting carefully and be as specific as possible: indicate instrumentation, orchestration, dynamics, key areas, rhythmic ostinatos, harmonic choices, etc.

Chapter Review

1   **Five-part rondos** have three distinct sections, labeled A, B, and C, and ordered as ABACA. The A sections in rondos are often called **refrains**. These are almost always in the tonic key, while the other sections are often in contrasting keys. In a rondo, one section might begin immediately after the previous section is over, or there might be a brief transition between sections.

2   Though sections in a rondo can be as short as just a couple of phrases, they can also be long enough to be in some kind of binary form, making the rondo itself a composite form (see Chapter 3).

3   While rondos often have five parts and can be understood in terms of the five-part rondo model, they just as often have more than five parts and can only be understood as some kind of expansion of that model. What binds all rondos together is an adherence to what is sometimes called the rondo principle: *primary thematic material is presented in alternation with multiple contrasting sections.*

4   As the name suggests, **sonata-rondos** are forms that combine elements of the rondo with elements of sonata form. In the sonata-rondo, the primary theme of the sonata form also assumes the role of the refrain in a rondo. The sonata-rondo can be thought of as a seven-part rondo with the first three parts grouped together to form an exposition, and the last three parts grouped together to form a recapitulation (see model). The music that occupies the fourth position of the rondo structure might sound like the development in a sonata form, it might

sound more like a contrasting C section in a rondo, or it might sound like a combination of both.

5   In the Baroque period and in earlier periods the refrain (A section) of a rondo was often just two phrases long; during that time it was also common to write rondos as independent pieces, though they were also used as movements in multi-movement works.

6   In the Classical period it became more common for the refrain of a rondo to be longer and in some kind of binary form, and the other sections were often longer as well. It became much less common for rondos to be written as independent pieces; rondos and sonata-rondos in the Classical period were often used as last movements in sonatas, symphonies, concertos, and chamber works.

7   The **concerto-rondo form** combines sonata form with rondo form, but unlike the sonata-rondo form, the material of the refrain is different than the material that serves as the primary theme of the sonata form and stands outside of the exposition and recapitulation (see model). The main thematic material in the first two refrains of a concerto-rondo is typically begun by the soloist and concluded by the orchestra. When the third refrain is present, its main thematic material is presented by either the soloist or the orchestra but generally not by both. The main thematic material in the final refrain is typically begun by the orchestra and concluded by the soloist.

appendix I
Formal Models

Simple Binary

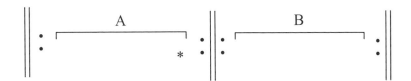

* If the first section ends with an authentic cadence in the home key, it's called **Sectional Binary**. If it ends with a half cadence, or if it cadences in a secondary key, it's called **Continuous Binary**.

Rounded Binary

* As above.

Balanced Binary

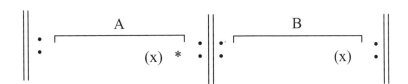

* As above; (x) = cadential material from the A section that returns to close the B section.

Ternary

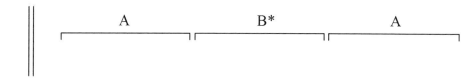

* The B section is usually in a contrasting key.

Sonata Form

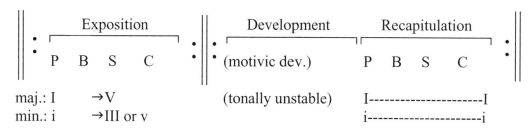

P = Primary Theme, B = Bridge, S = Secondary Theme, C = Closing (Roman numerals indicate key areas)

Fugue

Exposition	*Episode*	(followed by an alternation of
S enters, followed by **A**, followed by an alternation of S and A entries until all voices have entered	sequences and motivic development	Restatements and Episodes in various closely related keys until the music returns to the tonic key and the fugue ends)

S = Subject, A = Answer, Restatement = return of the subject in its entirety

Ritornello Form

Opening Ritornello	*Solo Section*	(followed by an alternation of
Ritornello theme presented by full orchestra in the tonic key	sequences and motivic development featuring soloist(s)	Ritornellos and Solo Sections in various closely related keys until the music returns to the tonic key and the movement ends)

Classical Concerto Form

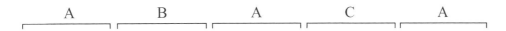

	Orch. Exposition	Solo Exposition	Development	Recapitulation
	P B (S) C	P B S C	(motivic dev.)	P B S C (w/cadenza)
maj.:	I--------------------I	→V	(unstable)	I---------------------------I
min.:	i--------------------i	→III or v		i---------------------------i

Orch.= Orchestral, P = Primary Theme, B = Bridge, S = Secondary Theme, C = Closing (Roman numerals indicate key areas)

Five-Part Rondo

A	B	A	C	A

Sonata-Rondo

	Exposition (= A B A)	Development* (=C)	Recapitulation (= A B A)
	P (Br) S (Cl) P		P (Br) S (Cl) P
maj.:	I →V I		I-----------------------------I
min.:	i →III or v i		i-----------------------------i

P = Primary Theme, Br = Bridge, S = Secondary Theme, Cl = Closing (Roman numerals indicate key areas)

* The development could be replaced by new contrasting thematic material.

appendix II

Making a Phrase Diagram

Things to include:

1   **Composer's name, the title of the composition, the location of the phrases, and the overall formal type.** Indicate movements if it's a multi-movement work, and if a complete movement is not being analyzed, also indicate the section.

2   **Phrase endings, cadences, and measure numbers.** Indicate the measure in which the *last note* of each phrase occurs, and label each cadence by type (PAC, IAC, HC, PC, or DC).

3   **Phrase labels.** Add lower case letters to each successive phrase (a, b, c, etc.), using a new letter for each phrase that sounds truly independent of those that came before it. If a phrase is an exact or almost exact repetition of an earlier phrase, use the earlier letter associated with that material; if it sounds like an altered version of an earlier phrase, use the earlier letter associated with that material and add either a number (a1, a2, etc.) or a prime symbol (a, a′, a″, etc.) to distinguish it.

4   **Phrase groupings.** Add brackets above groups of phrases that seem to go together. If the group is a period, double period, sentence, or phrase group, label it as such, and if it is a period or double period, specify whether it is parallel or contrasting.

5   **Formal labels and repeats.** Add any labels that are particular to the overall formal type (exposition, development, etc.) and also include repeat signs and end bars where they occur in the score.

6   **Modulations.** Add arrows and new key labels underneath a phrase marking if the phase modulates, using colons followed by upper-case letters for major keys/lower-case letters for minor ones (→A:, →g:, etc.).

7   **Sequences.** Add up/down arrows and Arabic numerals to denote harmonic sequence types underneath a phrase marking if a phrase is a sequence (↑5 seq., ↓3 seq., etc.). If the sequence spans a number of phrases, add a bracket above the phrase group and label the sequence type above the bracket.

- for D instruments, read the middle line as C (like an alto clef)
- for B♭ (or B) instruments, read the fourth line from the bottom as C (like tenor clef)
- for G instruments, read the top line as C
- for E♭ (or E) instruments, read the lines and spaces as you would in bass clef.

One way to quickly memorize this set of reading patterns is to notice how it is like an inversion of the lines in a bass clef:

FIGURE A.1

For example, a trumpet in B♭ sounds a major second lower than written, so a written D in their part will sounds as a C:

written in the B♭ trumpet part as

the sounding (concert) pitch is

FIGURE A.2

FIGURE A.3

Conductors reading the B♭ trumpet part can simply ignore the clef, replace the transposed key signature with the concert key signature, and read the lines and spaces as they sound (in this part, all a step lower than written):

written in the B♭ trumpet part as

conductor reads C

FIGURE A.4

FIGURE A.5

It is important to remember that one must ignore the key signature in the transposed part and assume the concert key signature instead. For example, if the concert key is D major, a part for clarinet in A will be written in F major; if that part has a written E, one must interpret the note on the bottom line as C♯ because the concert key is D major (ignoring the F major key signature in the transposed part):

the concert pitch is

written in the A clarinet part as

conductor reads C♯

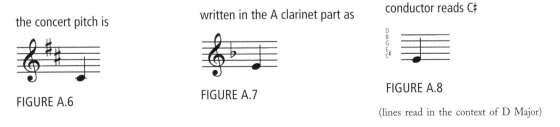

FIGURE A.6

FIGURE A.7

FIGURE A.8

(lines read in the context of D Major)

Not all scores are transposing; to avoid the difficulties of reading a transposed score, some composers write C scores that show all of the parts at their sounding pitch (rather than how they are written in the parts used by the players). When reading C scores, conductors must remember that those reading a part that transposes will be looking at a different set of notes than they are and phrase their comments in rehearsal accordingly. For example, "let me hear all those who play the repeated Ds in mm. 38–40" could be confusing for some of the musicians if those concert Ds were written as Ds in non-transposing parts, as Cs for those instruments in D, and as Fs for those instruments in A. It would better to say "let me hear all of the parts that have the repeated pedal tone in mm. 38–40."

appendix IV
Notes on the Audio Examples

Website Track Listing

Page numbers refer to corresponding scores in the *Anthology for Hearing Form*.

Page 1
Bach, J.S. Goldberg Variations, Aria. Jeno Jando, piano. Naxos Cat. # 8.557268.

Page 2
Bach, J.S. Two-Part Inventions, No. 1 in C Major. Janos Sebestyen, piano. Naxos Cat. # 8.550679.

Page 3
Bach, J.S. Two-Part Inventions, No. 13 in A minor. Janos Sebestyen, piano. Naxos Cat. # 8.550679.

Page 4
Bach, J.S. Well-Tempered Clavier, Book I, C Major Prelude. Jeno Jando, piano. Naxos Cat. # 8.553796–9.

Page 5
Bach, J.S. Well-Tempered Clavier, Book I, Fugue in F Major. Jeno Jando, piano. Naxos Cat. # 8.553796–97.

Page 7
Bach, J.S. Well-Tempered Clavier, Book I, Fugue in B Major. Jeno Jando, piano. Naxos Cat. # 8.553796–97.

Page 9
Bach, J.S. Well-Tempered Clavier, Book II, Fugue in E Minor. Jeno Jando, piano. Naxos Cat. # 8.550970–71.

Page 13

Bach, J.S. Orchestral Suite No. 2, Badinerie. Capella Istropolitana; Jaroslav Dvorak. Naxos Cat. # 8.550244.

Page 14

Bach, J.S. Orchestral Suite No. 3, Air. Capella Istropolitana; Jaroslav Dvorak. Naxos Cat. # 8.550245.

Page 16

Bach, J.S. Orchestral Suite No. 3, Gavotte I. Capella Istropolitana; Jaroslav Dvorak. Naxos Cat. # 8.554043.

Page 18

Bach, J.S. Orchestral Suite No. 3, Gavotte II. Capella Istropolitana; Jaroslav Dvorak. Naxos Cat. # 8.554043.

Page 20

Bach, J.S. Mass in B Minor, "Crucifixus". Christian Brembeck; Capella Istropolitana; Hartmut Elbert; Martina Koppelstetter; Jan Rozehnal; Faridah Schafer Subrata; Markus Schafer; Slovak Philharmonic Chorus; Friederike Wagner. Naxos Cat. # 8.550585–86.

Page 24

Bach, J.S. Brandenburg Concerto No. 1, I. Cologne Chamber Orchestra; Helmut Muller-Bruhl. Naxos Cat. # 8.554607.

Page 34

Beethoven, L. v. Piano Sonata No. 1 in F Minor, I. Alfred Brendel, piano. Vox Cat. # CDX-5056 courtesy of Naxos of America.

Page 38

Beethoven, L. v. Piano Sonata, No. 8 in C minor, Op. 13, III. Jeno Jando, piano. Naxos Cat. # 8.550045.

Page 44

Beethoven, L. v. Symphony No. 2 in D Major, IV. Zagreb Philharmonic Orchestra; Richard Edlinger. Naxos Cat. # 8.550177.

Page 64

Beethoven, L. v. Symphony No. 3 in E-Flat Major, I. Belgian Radio and Television Philharmonic Orchestra; Alexander Rahbari. Naxos Cat. # 8.550407.

Page 97

Beethoven. Symphony No. 5 in C Minor, I. Nicolaus Esterhazy Sinfonia; Bela Drahos. Naxos Cat. # 8.554061.

Page 113

Beethoven, L. v. String Quartet, Op. 131, I. Kodaly Quartet. Naxos Cat. # 8.554594.

Page 116

Brahms, J. Variations on a Theme by Haydn. London Philharmonic Orchestra; Marin Alsop. Naxos Cat. # 8.557430.

Page 154

Brahms, J. Symphony No. 4 in E Minor, IV. London Philharmonic Orchestra; Marin Alsop. Naxos Cat. # 8.570230.

Page 185

Brahms, J. Concerto for Violin in D Major, Op. 77, I. Ilya Kaler, violin; Bournemouth Symphony Orchestra; Pietari Inkinen, conducting. Naxos Cat. # 8.570321.

Page 219

Chopin, F. Prelude in E Minor. Idil Biret, piano. Naxos Cat. # 8.554046.

Page 220

Handel, G.F. Giulio Cesare, I/5, "Non Disperar". Angelo Bonazzoli; Patrizia Bozzo; Il Concento Ecclesiastico; Luca Franco Ferrari; Angelo Galeano; Angelo Manzotti; Paola Pittaluga; Guido Ripoli; Riccardo Ristori; Alexandra Zabala Concerto Cat. # CD 2042–3 courtesy of Naxos of America.

Page 222

Handel, G.F. Giulio Cesare, I/6, "L'empio, sleale, indegno". Angelo Bonazzoli; Patrizia Bozzo; Il Concento Ecclesiastico; Luca Franco Ferrari; Angelo Galeano; Angelo Manzotti; Paola Pittaluga; Guido Ripoli; Riccardo Ristori; Alexandra Zabala. Concerto Cat. # CD 2042–3. courtesy of Naxos of America.

Page 226

Handel, G.F. Messiah, Part I, Overture. Owen Burdick; Trinity Church Choir, New York; Trinity Church Orchestra. Naxos Cat. # 8.554511–12.

Page 230

Haydn, J. Piano Sonata No. 33 in C Minor, Hob. XVI: 20, I. Jeno Jando, piano. Naxos Cat. # 8.553800.

Page 236

Haydn, J. Piano Sonata No. 50 in D Major, Hob. XVI/37, III. Jeno Jando, piano. Naxos Cat. # 8.553128.

Page 239

Haydn, J. Symphony No. 101 in D Major, IV. Capella Istropolitana; Barry Wordsworth. Naxos Cat. # 8.553222.

Page 258

Haydn, J. Symphony No. 103 in E-Flat Major, I. Capella Istropolitana; Barry Wordsworth. Naxos Cat. # 8.550387.

Page 276

Mozart, W.A. Piano Sonata in A major, K. 331, I. Jeno Jando, piano. Naxos Cat. # 8.550448.

Page 282

Mozart, W.A. Piano Sonata in B-Flat, K. 333, III. Jeno Jando, piano. Naxos Cat. # 8.550449.

Page 288

Mozart, W.A. Eine kleine Nachtmusik, K. 525 (All 4 Movements). Petter Sundkvist; Swedish Chamber Orchestra. Naxos Cat. # 8.557023.

Page 300

Mozart, W.A. Symphony No. 35 in D Major, IV. Capella Istropolitana; Barry Wordsworth. Naxos Cat. # 8.550186.

Page 315

Mozart, W.A. Symphony No. 40 in G Minor, I. Capella Istropolitana; Barry Wordsworth. Naxos Cat. # 8.55016.

Page 333

Mozart, W.A. Symphony No. 40 in G Minor, III, Menuetto. Capella Istropolitana; Barry Wordsworth. Naxos Cat. # 8.550164.

Page 335

Mozart, W.A. Piano Concerto in D Major, K. 107, I. Gerrit Zitterbart, piano; Schlierbacher Chamber Orchestra; Thomas Fey, conducting. Haennsler Cat. # CD98.149. courtesy of Naxos of America.

Page 344

Mozart, W.A. Piano Concerto in E-flat Major, K. 271, I. Jeno Jando, piano; Concentus Hungaricus; Andras Ligeti, conducting. Naxos Cat. # 8.550203.

Page 373

Purcell, H. Dido and Aeneas, "When I Am Laid in Earth". Kym Amps; Scholars Baroque Ensemble. Naxos Cat. # 8.556839.

Page 376

Vivaldi, A. The Four Seasons, Concerto No. 2 ("Summer"), I. Cho-Liang Lin, violin; Anthony Newman, harpsichord; Sejong. Naxos Cat. # 8.557920.

Page 389

Vivalid, A. The Four Seasons, Concerto No. 4 ("Winter"), I. Cho-Liang Lin, violin; Anthony Newman, harpsichord; Sejong. Naxos Cat. # 8.557920.

Bibliography

Anthologies for Musical Analysis

Burkhart, Charles. *Anthology for Musical Analysis*. 6th ed. Belmont, CA: Thomson-Schirmer, 2004.

Kostka, Stefan and Roger Graybill. *Anthology of Music for Analysis*. Upper Saddle River, NJ: Pearson Prentice Hall, 2004.

Stein, Leon. *Anthology of Musical Forms*. New York: Warner Bros., 1962

Turek, Ralph. *Analytical Anthology of Music*. 2nd ed. New York: McGraw-Hill, 1992.

Textbooks

Berry, Wallace. *Form in Music: An Examination of Traditional Techniques of Musical Structure and their Application in Historical and Contemporary Styles*. 2nd ed. Englewood Cliffs, NJ: Prentice-Hall, Inc., 1986.

Fontaine, Paul. *Basic Formal Structures in Music*. New York: Meredith Publishing Company, 1967.

Gauldin, Robert. *A Practical Approach to Eighteenth-Century Counterpoint*. Prospect Heights, IL: Waveland Press, 1995. Originally published Englewood Cliffs, NJ: Prentice-Hall, 1988.

Green, Douglass. *Form in Tonal Music: An Introduction to Analysis*. 2nd ed. New York: Holt, Rinehart and Winston, 1979.

Kohs, Ellis. *Musical Form: Studies in Analysis and Synthesis*. Boston: Houghton Mifflin Company, 1976.

Mathes, James. *The Analysis of Musical Form*. Upper Saddle River, NJ: Pearson Prentice Hall, 2007.

Morris, R. O. *The Structure of Music*. London: Oxford University Press, 1935.

Spencer, Peter and Peter Temko. *A Practical Approach to the Study of Form in Music*. Prospect Heights, IL: Waveland Press Inc., 1994. Originally published Englewood Cliffs, NJ: Prentice-Hall (Simon & Schuster), 1988.

Spring, Glenn and Jere T. Hutchison. *Musical Form and Analysis*. New York: McGraw-Hill, 1994.

Stein, Leon. *Structure and Style: The Study and Analysis of Musical Forms*. Expanded edition. Evanston, IL: Summy-Birchard, 1979.

Related Literature

Adrian, Jack. "The Function of the Apparent Tonic at the Beginning of Development Sections." *Intégral* 5 (1991), 1–53.

Andrews, Harold. "The Submediant in Haydn's Development Sections." In *Haydn Studies* (New York: Norton, 1981).

Arthurs, Daniel. "Applying Traditional and Proportional Aspects of Form to Atonal Music." *Journal of Music Theory Pedagogy* 18 (2004), 1–21.

Bartha, Dénes. "On Beethoven's Thematic Structures." *Musical Quarterly* 61 (1970), 759–778.

——. "Song Form and the Concept of 'Quatrain.'" In *Haydn Studies* (New York: Norton, 1981).

Batt, Robert. "Function and Structure of Transitions in Sonata–Form Music of Mozart." *Canadian University Music Review* 9 (1988), 157–201.

Beach, David. "Schubert's Experiments with Sonata Form: Formal–Tonal Design Versus Underlying Structure." *Music Theory Spectrum* 15/1 (1993), 1–18.

——. "Phrase Expansion: Three Analytical Studies." *Music Analysis* 14 (1995), 27–47.

Blombach, Ann. "Phrase and Cadence: A Study of Terminology and Definition." *Journal of Music Theory Pedagogy* 1 (1987), 225–251.

Bonds, Mark Evan. "Haydn's False Recapitulations and the Perception of Sonata Form in the Eighteenth Century." Ph.D. diss.: Harvard University, 1988.

——. *Wordless Rhetoric: Musical Form and the Metaphor of the Oration.* Cambridge, MA: Harvard University Press, 1991.

Broyles, Michael. "Organic Form and the Binary Repeat." *Musical Quarterly* 66 (1980), 339–360.

Budday, Wolfgang. *Grundlagen musicalischer Formen der Wiener Klassik: An Hand der zeitgenössischen Theorie von Joseph Riepel und Heinrich Koch dargestellt an Menuetten und Sonatensätzen (1750–1790).* Kassel: Bärenreiter, 1983.

Cadwallader, Allen. "Form and Tonal Process." In *Trends in Schenkerian Research* (New York: Schirmer, 1990), 1–21.

Caplin, William. *Classical Form: A Theory of Formal Functions for the Instrumental Music of Haydn, Mozart, and Beethoven.* London: Oxford University Press, 1998.

——. "The 'Expanded Cadential Progression': A Category for the Analysis of Classical Form." *Journal of Musicological Research* 7 (1987), 215–257.

——. "Structural Expansion in Beethoven's Symphonic Forms." In *Beethoven's Compositional Process* (Lincoln: University of Nebraska Press, 1991), 27–54.

——. "Hybrid Themes: Toward a Refinement in the Classification of Classical Theme Types." *Beethoven Forum* 3 (1994), 151–165.

Cavett–Dunsby, Esther. *Mozart's Variations Reconsidered: Four Case Studies (K. 613, K. 501, K. 421/417b, K. 491).* New York: Garland, 1989.

Churgin, Bathia. "Harmonic and Tonal Instability in the Second Key Area of Classical Soanta Form." In *Convention in Eighteenth- and Nineteenth-Century Music: Essays in Honor of Leonard G. Ratner* (Stuyvesant, NY: Pendragon, 1992), 23–57.

Cole, Malcolm. "Haydn's Symphonic Rondo Finales; Their Structure and Stylistic Evolution." *Haydn Yearbook* 13 (1982), 113–142.

Cone, Edward T. *Musical Form and Musical Performance.* New York: Norton, 1968.

Dahlhaus, Carl. "Some models of unity in musical form." *Journal of Music Theory* 19/1 (1975), 2–30.

——. "Satz und Periode: Zur Theorie der musikalischen Syntax." *Zeitschrift für Musiktheorie* 9 (1978), 16–26.

Darcy, Warren. "Bruckner's Sonata Deformations." *Bruckner Studies* (New York: Cambridge University Press, 1997), 256–277.

——— . "Rotational Form, Teleological Genesis, and Fantasy—Projection in the Slow Movement of Mahler's Sixth Symphony." *19th–Century Music* 25/1 (2001), 49–74.

Davis, Shelly. "H. C. Koch, the Classic Concerto, and the Sonata-Form Retransition." *Journal of Musicology* 2 (1983), 45–61.

Fillion, Michelle. "Sonata–Exposition Procedures in Haydn's Keyboard Sonatas." In *Haydn Studies* (New York: Norton, 1981), 475–481.

Folse, Stuart. "Popular Music as a Pedagogical Resource for Musicianship: Contextual Listening, Prolongations, Mediant Relationships, and Musical Form." *Journal of Music Theory Pedagogy* 18 (2004), 65–79.

Fisher, Steven. "Sonata Procedures in Haydn's Symphonic Rondo Finales of the 1770s." In *Haydn Studies* (New York: Norton, 1981), 481–487.

Forster, Robert. "Zur Funktion von Anfangsritornell und Reprise in den Kopfsätzen einiger Klavierkonzerte Mozarts." *Mozart–Jahrbuch 1986*, 74–89.

Frisch, Walter. *Brahms and the Principle of Developing Variation*. Berkeley: University of California Press, 1984.

Gagné, David. "The Compositional Use of Register in Three Piano Sonatas by Mozart." In *Trends in Schenkerian Research* (New York: Schirmer, 1990), 23–40.

Galand, Joel. "Form, Genre, and Style in the Eighteenth–Century Rondo." *Music Theory Spectrum* 17/1 (1995), 27–52.

——— . "Formenlehre Revived." *Intégral* 13 (1999), 143–200.

——— . "The Large–Scale Formal Role of the Solo Entry Theme in the Eighteenth-Century Concerto." *Journal of Music Theory* 44/2 (2000), 381–450.

Graybill, Roger. "Brahms's Three–Key Expositions: Their Place within the Classical Tradition." Ph.D. diss.: Yale University, 1983.

——— . "Sonata Form and Reicha's Grande Coupe Binaire of 1814." *Theoria* 4 (1989), 89–105.

Haimo, Ethan. "Haydn's Altered Reprise." *Journal of Music Theory* 32 (1988), 335–351.

——— . *Haydn's Symphonic Forms: Essays in Compositional Logic*. Oxford: Clarendon Press, 1995.

Harutunian, John. "Haydn and Mozart: Tonic–Dominant Polarity in Mature Sonata-Style Works." *Journal of Musicological Research* 9 (1990), 273–298.

Hepokoski, James. "Structural Tensions in Sibelius's Fifth Symphony: Circular Stasis, Linear Progress, and the Problem of 'Traditional' Form." *Sibelius Forum* (Helsinki: Sibelius–Akatemia, 1998), 213–236.

——— . "Back and Forth From Egmont: Beethoven, Mozart, and the Nonresolving Recapitulation." *19th-Century Music* 25/2–3 (2002), 127–164.

——— . "Beyond the Sonata Principle." *Journal of the American Musicological Society* 55/1 (2002), 91–154.

Hepokoski, James and Warren Darcy. "The Medial Caesura and Its Role in the Eighteenth-Century Sonata Exposition." *Music Theory Spectrum* 19/2 (1997), 115–154.

——— . *Elements of Sonata Theory*. New York: Oxford University Press, 2006.

Hopkins, Robert. "When a Coda is More than a Coda: Reflections on Beethoven." In *Explorations in Music, the Arts, and Ideas: Essays in Honor of Leonard B. Meyer* (Stuyvesant, NY: Pendragon, 1988), 393–410.

Jackson, Timothy. "Brucknerian Models: Sonata Form and Linked Internal Auxiliary Cadences." *Sibelius Forum II* (Helsinki: Sibelius–Akatemia, 2003).

——— . "The Finale of Bruckner's Seventh Symphony and Tragic Reversed Sonata Form." *Bruckner Studies* (New York: Cambridge University, 1997), 140–208.

——— . "The Tragic Reversed Recapitulation in the German Classical Tradition." *Journal of Music Theory* 40/1 (1996), 61–111.

Jan, Steven. "X Marks the Spot: Schenkerian Perspectives on the Minor-Key Classical Development Section." *Music Analysis* 11 (1992), 37–54.

Küster, Konrad. *Formale Aspekte ds ersten Allegros in Mozarts Konzerten.* Kassel: Bärenreiter, 1991.

Larsen, Jens Peter. "Sonata Form Problems." In *Handel, Haydn, and the Viennese Classical Style,* trans. Ulrich Krämer (Ann Arbor: University of Michigan Press, 1988), 269–279

LaRue, Jan. "Bifocal Tonality in Haydn Symphonies." In *Convention in Eighteenth- and Nineteenth-Century Music: Essays in Honor of Leonard G. Ratner* (Stuyvesant, NY: Pendragon, 1992), 59–73.

——. *Guidelines for Style Analysis.* 2nd ed. Warren, MI: Harmonie Park Press, 1992.

Lester, Joel. *Compositional Theory in the Eighteenth Century.* Cambridge, MA: Harvard University Press, 1992.

Levy, Janet. "Gesture, Form, and Syntax in Haydn's Music." In *Haydn Studies* (New York: Norton, 1981), 355–362.

Longyear, Rey and Kate Covington. "Sources of the Three-Key Exposition." *Journal of Musicology* 6 (1988), 448–470.

Marston, Nicholas. "The Recapitulation–Transition in Mozart's Music." In *Mozart–Jahrbuch 1991,* 793–809.

Marx, Adolph Bernhard. *Musical Form in the Age of Beethoven: Selected Writings on Theory and Method.* New York: Cambridge University Press, 1997.

Ratner, Leonard. *Classic Music: Expression, Form, and Style.* New York: Schirmer, 1980.

Rosen, Charles. *The Classical Style: Haydn, Mozart, Beethoven.* New York: Norton, 1972.

——. *Sonata Forms.* Revised ed. New York: W.W. Norton, 1988.

——. "Schubert's Inflections of Classical Form." The Cambridge Companion to Schubert (New York: Cambridge University Press, 1997), 72–98.

Rothstein, William. *Phrase Rhythm in Tonal Music.* New York: Schirmer, 1989.

Schachter, Carl. "Analysis by Key: Another Look at Modulation." *Music Analysis* 6 (1987), 289–318.

Schenker, Heinrich. *Free Composition.* Ed. and trans. by Ernst Oster. New York: Longman, 1979.

Schmalfeldt, Janet. "Cadential Processes: The Evaded Cadence and the 'One More Time' Technique." *Journal of Musicological Research* 12 (1992), 1–51.

——. "Towards a Reconciliation of Schenkerian Concepts with Traditional and Recent Theories of Form." *Music Analysis* 10 (1991), 233–287.

Shamgar, Beth. "On Locating the Retransition in Classic Sonata Form." *Music Review* 42 (1981), 130–143.

Sisman, Elaine. "Small and Expanded Forms: Koch's Model and Haydn's Music." *Musical Quarterly* 68 (1982), 444–475.

——. *Haydn and the Classical Variation.* Cambridge, MA: Harvard University Press, 1993.

Sly, Gordon. "Schubert's Innovations in Sonata Form: Compositional Logic and Structural Interpretation." *Journal of Music Theory* 45/1 (2001), 119–143; 147–150.

Smyth, David. "Balanced Interruption and the Formal Repeat." *Music Theory Spectrum* 15/1 (1993), 76–88.

——. "Large–Scale Rhythm and Classical Form." *Music Theory Spectrum* 12/2 (1990), 236–246.

Snyder, John. "Schenker and the First Movement of Mozart's Sonata, K. 545: An Uninterrupted Sonata-Form Movement." *Theory and Practice* 16 (1991), 51–78.

Stevens, Jane. "Patterns of Recapitulation in the First Movements of Mozart's Piano Concertos." In *Musical Humanism and Its Legacy: Essays in Honor of Claude Palisca* (Stuyvesant, NY: Pendragon, 1992), 397–418.

Swain, Joseph. "Form and Function of the Classical Cadenza." *Journal of Musicology* 6 (1988), 27–59.

Tovey, Donald. *The Forms of Music*. New York: Meridian, 1956.

Webster, James. "Schubert's Sonata Form and Brahms' First Maturity." *Nineteenth Century Music* 2 (1978), 18–35 and *Nineteenth Century Music* 3 (1979), 52–71.

——. "Freedom of Form in Haydn's Early String Quartets." In *Haydn Studies* (New York: Norton, 1981), 522–530.

——. *Haydn's "Farewell" Symphony and the Idea of Classical Style: Through-Composition and Cyclic Integration in His Instrumental Music*. Cambridge: Cambridge University Press, 1991.

Wolf, Eugene. "The Recapitulations in Haydn's London Symphonies." *Musical Quarterly* 52 (1966), 71–89.

Reference

Perone, James E. *Form and Analysis Theory: A Bibliography*. Westport, CN: Greenwood Press, 1998.

Index

Workbook for
Hearing Form

Matthew Santa

Name: _____

Homework Assignment 1.1: Listen to the theme (marked "Aria" in the score) from J. S. Bach's Goldberg Variations while following along with the score, and mark cadence points in the score as you listen. Then choose the incomplete phrase diagram below that most closely matches the number of cadences you heard, and fill in the blanks of that diagram with cadence types, sequence types, measure numbers or key areas, as appropriate (blanks after arrows are for keys). Next, look at the incomplete phrase diagram that did not reflect your initial hearing, and fill in the blanks of that diagram. Finally, listen again while following this latter diagram and see if you can understand the logic behind the other interpretation.

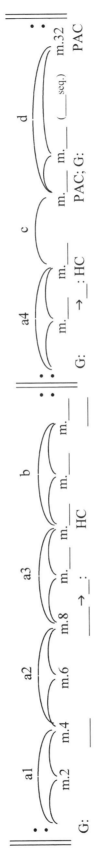

Interpretation #1

a1   a2   a3   b

m.2   m.4   m.6   m.8   m.___   m.___   m.___

G: ___   →__: HC

a4   c   d

m.___   m.___   m.___ (___seq.)   m.32

G: →__:HC   PAC; G: PAC

OR

Interpretation #2

a1   a2   a3   b   a4   a5   c1   c2

m.2   m.4   m.6   m.8   m.___   m.___   m.___

G: →__: IAC→G: ___   →__: HC

a6   d   e   f   g

m.___   m.___   m.___ (___seq.)   m.32

G: →__:HC   PAC; G: PC   PAC

Name: _____

Homework Assignment 1.2: Listen to Schubert's "Kennst du das Land?" (*Mignon*, D. 321) without the score while conducting along in 2/4. Use the steady meter and measure numbers to follow along with the diagram below. Then fill in the blanks of the diagram with cadence types, measure numbers or key areas, as appropriate, and answer the questions at the bottom of the page. Finally, listen again while following this diagram and see if you can understand the logic behind the interpretive choices that differed from your own.

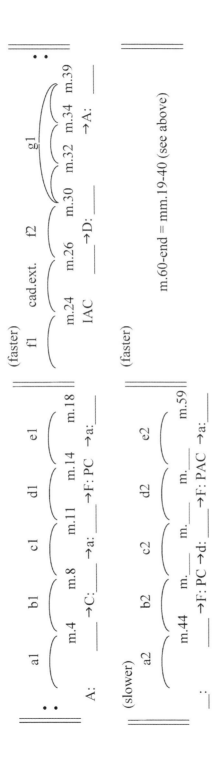

1. The rolled chord in m. 17 is composed of the notes F, A, B, and D♯. What kind of harmony is this? _____

2. The material in mm. 31–34 is composed of two melodically independent units. Why are these two units considered subphrases here and not phrases? _____

Name: _____

Homework Assignment 3.1: Listen to the Menuetto from Mozart's Symphony No. 40, III while following along with the score, and mark cadence points in the score as you listen. Choose the incomplete phrase diagram below that most closely matches the number of cadences you heard, fill in the blanks of that diagram with cadence types, measure numbers or key areas, as appropriate (blanks after arrows are for keys), and answer the question at the bottom of the page. Next, look at the incomplete phrase diagram that did not reflect your initial hearing, and fill in the blanks of that diagram. Finally, listen again while following this latter diagram and see if you can understand the logic behind the other interpretation.

Interpretation #1

a1   a2   a3   a4   a5   cad.ext.   a6

m.3   m.6   m.___   m.___   m.___   m.26   m.___   m.36   m.___   m.42

g: IAC   →___: PAC   B♭:   →g: IAC   ___   ___   PAC

OR

Interpretation #2

a1   a2   a3   b   a4   a5   a6   c   a7   cad.ext.   a8   a9

m.3   m.6   m.___   m.___   m.___   m.___   m.26   m.___   m.36   m.___   m.42

g: IAC   →___: PAC   B♭:   →g: IAC →E♭:   →g: →d: HC →g: PAC

What is the form of the Menuetto? _____ form (Note that the music in mm. 36–42 should be considered a coda and thus not part of the body of the form.)

Homework Assignment 3.2: Listen to the aria from Handel's *Giulio Cesare*, Act I, Scene 5 ("Non disperar") while following along with the score, and mark cadence points in the score as you listen (NB: note that the bass line of the score often changes to tenor clef). The incomplete phrase diagram given below may or may not reflect your interpretation. Fill in the blanks of the diagram with cadence types, measure numbers or key areas, as appropriate, and answer the question at the bottom of the page, taking care to note the differences between your own interpretation and the one suggested below. Finally, listen again while following this diagram and see if you can understand the logic behind the interpretive choices that differed from your own.

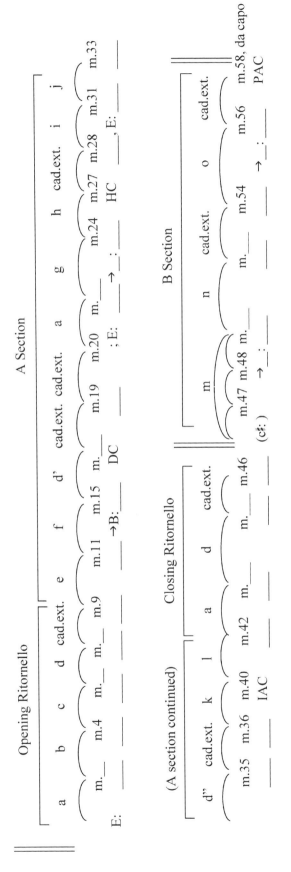

A Section

Opening Ritornello

Closing Ritornello

(A section continued)

B Section

What is the form of this aria? _____ form (Note that the ritornellos are considered part of the A section.)

Name: _____

Homework Assignment 3.3: Listen to the Gavotte II from J. S. Bach's Orchestral Suite No. 3 in D major, while listening and conducting without the score and following the incomplete phrase diagram below (it is conducted in 2, and starts on beat 2). Then fill in the blanks of the diagram with cadence types, sequence types, measure numbers or key areas, as appropriate, and answer the questions at the bottom of the page, taking care to note any differences between your own interpretation and the one suggested below. Finally, check your work against the score, and listen again while following this diagram to see if you can understand the logic behind any interpretive choices that differed from your own.

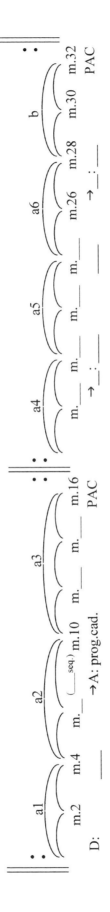

al
m.2

a2
m.4   m.___ (___seq.) m.10
    ___   →A: prog.cad.
D:

a3
m.___   m.___   m.16
              PAC

a4
m.___   m.___
→_:___

a5
m.___   m.___

a6
m.26   m.28

b
m.30   m.32
→_:___   PAC

What is the form of the Gavotte II? _____ form. The Gavottes I and II are intended to be performed as a single movement with a *da capo* after the Gavotte II. What is the overall form of that movement? _____ form

Name: _____

Homework Assignment 3.4: Listen to the third movement from Mozart's *Eine kleine Nachtmusik* without the score while conducting along in 3/4. Use the steady meter and the repeat scheme to follow along with the diagram below. Then fill in the blanks of the diagram with cadence types, measure numbers or key areas, as appropriate, and answer the questions at the bottom of the page, taking care to note any differences between your own interpretation and the one suggested below. Finally, check your work against the score, and listen again while following this diagram to see if you can understand the logic behind any interpretive choices that differed from your own.

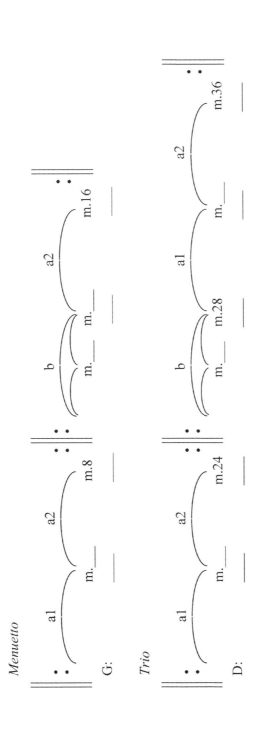

What is the form of the Menuetto? _____ _____ form

Measures 6 and 7 sound as though they are a single measure of 3/2, creating a 3-against-2 feel. What is this effect called? _____

What is the form of the Trio? _____ _____ form

What is the overall form of the movement when the *da capo* marking is observed? _____ _____ form

Homework Assignment 3.5: Listen to Josephine Lang's "Oh ich manchmal dein Gedanke" without the score while conducting along in 3/4. Use the steady meter to follow along with the diagram below. Then fill in the blanks of the diagram with cadence types, measure numbers or key areas, as appropriate, and follow the instructions in the paragraph that follows it. Finally, listen again while following this diagram and see if you can understand the logic behind any interpretive choices that differed from your own.

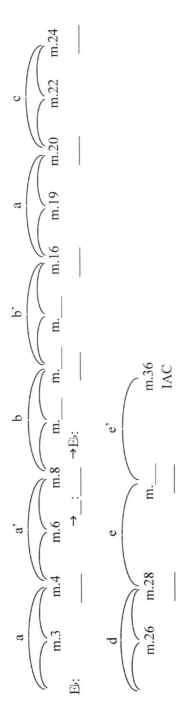

The very first phrase in this song is interesting in that the piano part serves as a bridge connecting its two subphrases. What specifically about the piano part on beat 3 of m. 2 makes it sound like such an indispensible continuation of the vocal part in that same measure?

One could view this as a ternary form with a modified return of A (ABA') or as a rounded binary form without any repeats. Add the formal labels A B and A' to the phrase diagram above the phrase where those sections start. Then read about the differences between rounded binary forms and ternary forms on pp. 35–36 of your textbook, and write a paragraph arguing for either a rounded binary or a ternary interpretation (there is no single right answer).

Name: _____

Homework Assignment 3.6: Listen to the first twenty-three measures of the Courante from Elisabeth Jacquet de la Guerre's *Pièces de clavecin* while following along with the score, and mark cadence points in the score as you listen. Then choose the incomplete phrase diagram below that most closely matches the number of cadences you heard, and fill in the blanks of that diagram with cadence types, sequence types, measure numbers or key areas, as appropriate (blanks after arrows are for keys). Next, look at the incomplete phrase diagram that did not reflect your initial hearing, fill in the blanks of that diagram, and answer the questions at the bottom of the page. Finally, listen again while following this latter diagram and see if you can understand the logic behind the other interpretation.

Interpretation #1

OR

Interpretation #2

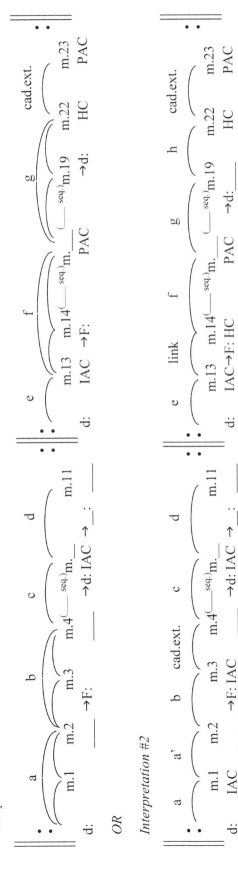

NB: The "Double" that follows m. 23 is simply an embellished version of mm. 1–23 and shares an identical phrase structure. In performance, one would play the A section in mm. 1–11, then the A section of the Double, then the B section in mm. 12–23, then the B section of the Double.

What is the form of the Courante? _____ _____ form

This movement interprets 3/2 as a compound duple meter, but measure 10 sounds as though it is in a simple triple meter, creating a 3-against-2 feel. What is this effect called? _____ In what measure does this effect return? _____

Name: _____

Homework Assignment 4.1: Listen to the first movement from Haydn's Sonata in C minor, Hob. XVI: 20 while following along with the score, and mark cadence points in the score as you listen. The incomplete phrase diagram given below may or may not reflect your interpretation. Fill in the blanks with formal labels (e.g. exposition, primary theme, bridge, etc.), cadence types, sequence types, measure numbers or key areas, as appropriate (blanks before colons are for keys), and answer the question at the bottom of the page, taking care to note the differences between your own interpretation and the one suggested below. Finally, listen again while following this diagram and see if you can understand the logic behind the interpretive choices that differed from your own. Note that there is no bridge in the recapitulation!

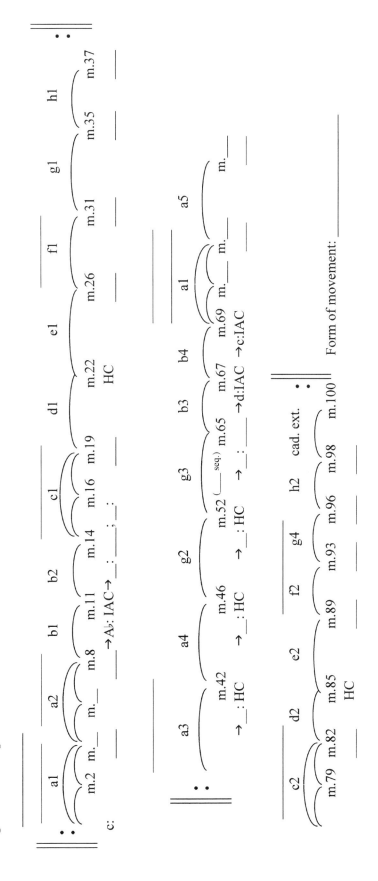

Name: _____

Homework Assignment 4.2: Listen to the development section from the first movement of Beethoven's Symphony No. 3 while following along with the score, and mark cadence points in the score as you listen. The incomplete phrase diagram given below may or may not reflect your interpretation. Fill in the blanks with cadence types, sequence types, measure numbers or key areas, as appropriate (blanks after arrows are for keys), and answer the question at the end.

h	b4	b5	b6	a4	a5	a6	link	a7	i1	i2	i3
m.154bis	m.166	m.170	m.174	m.___	m.181	m.185	m.193	m.198	m.205	m.209	m.213 (___ seq.) m.___
→C:HC		____	c:IAC	→c#:HC	→__:HC	HC		→__:	→c:HC	→f:HC	→Ab:

b7	b8	b9	b10	j1	j2	j3	k1	k2	k3	e5	e6
m.224	m.___	m.___	m.___	m.239	m.___	m.247	m.259	m.271	m.284	m.288	m.292
IAC	HC	IAC	→__:PAC	→c:IAC	→g:IAC	→d:IAC	→a:IAC	→b:HC	→ __:		→ __:

e7	e8	cad. ext.	link	a9	link	e9	e10	e11	e12	ℓ1
m.___	m.300	m.308	m.312	m.316	m.320	m.322	m.330	m.___	m.338	m.345
→C:IAC		IAC; c: IAC	IAC	→ Eb: IAC; eb:		→ __:	m.___ → __:		→eb: ____	IAC

ℓ2	ℓ3	ℓ4
m.353	m.361	m.398
→ __:IAC	→eb: ____	IAC

What kind of harmonic sequence is formed by the succession of phrases ℓ1 and ℓ2? _____

Name: _____

Homework Assignment 4.3: Listen to the first movement from Haydn, Symphony No. 103 while following along with the score, and mark cadence points in the score as you listen. Fill in the blanks with formal labels (e.g. exposition, primary theme, bridge, etc.), cadence types, sequence types, measure numbers or key areas, as appropriate.

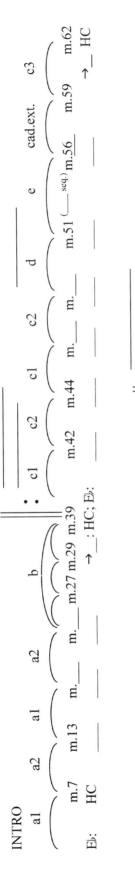

INTRO

a1 a2 a1 a2 a2 ⌢ c1 c2 c1 d e cad.ext. c3

m.7 m.13 m.___ m.___ m.27 m.29 m.39 m.42 m.44 m.___ m.___ m.51 ⌢seq.⌣ m.56 m.59 m.62

E♭: HC ___ ___ → ___ : HC; E♭: → ___ : HC ___ → ___ HC

(No Closing!)

c4 c5 f1 g1 g2 cad.ext. ‖ c6 c7 h link g3

m.___ m.___ m.79 m.83 m.92 m.94 m.101⌢seq.⌣ m.112 m.131 m.___ m.___ m.___

PAC HC m.___ PAC PAC →f: HC (106-108)→c:HC →f: IAC →D♭:

(No Closing!)

g4 c1 c2 c1 c2 c1 d e cad.ext. g5 g6

m.___ ⌢seq.⌣ m.159 m.161 m.163 m.___ m.___ m.___ ⌢seq.⌣ m.___ m.179 m.___ m.___ m.201

→E♭:HC ___ ___ ___ HC ___ ___

CODA

a1 a2 f2 c8 cad. ext.

m.208 m.214 m.220 m.227 end ‖

HC ___ ___ Form of movement: _____

Name: _____

Homework Assignment 4.4: Listen to the first movement from Mozart's *Eine kleine Nachtmusik* while following along with the score, and mark cadence points in the score as you listen. The incomplete phrase diagram given below may or may not reflect your interpretation. Fill in the blanks with formal labels (e.g. exposition, primary theme, bridge, etc.), cadence types, measure numbers, or key areas, as appropriate.

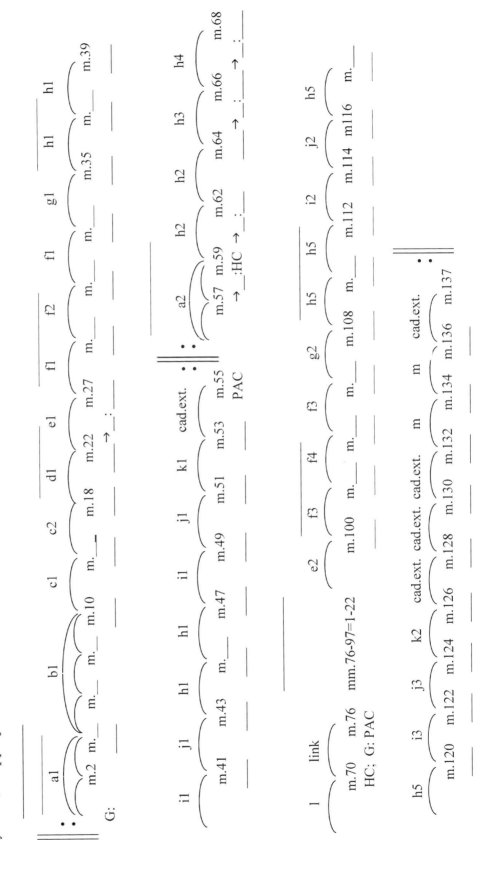

Homework Assignment 4.5: Listen to the first movement of Beethoven's Piano Sonata, Op. 13 and mark its phrase structure directly on the score. Then look at the incomplete phrase diagram below; this diagram may or may not reflect your interpretation. Fill in the blanks with formal labels related to sonata form (e.g. Exposition, Primary Theme, Bridge, etc.), cadence types, measure numbers or key areas, as appropriate. Then answer the questions that follow the diagram.

Introduction

```
                                                                              _____  _____
a1  a2  a3  a4  b1  a5  a6  a7  b2  b3  c1  c2  d1  d1  e1  e2
                                                                              m.39  m.43
       m.__  m.__  m.4  m.5  m.6  m.7  m.9  m.9  m.11  m.__  m.__  m.__  m.35  →_:‖  (elis.)
  c:   HC   IAC   HC →E♭:prog  ___  HC →D:___  →c: HC  ___  DC   PAC   ___  →_:‖  →_:‖

                                                                    _____  _____  _____
e3  link  f1  g1  f2  g2  f3  g3  g4  g5  cad.ext.  h1  h2  i1  i2  c3  link
                                                                    ‖:
       m.49  m.51  m.55  m.59  m.63  m.67  m.71  m.75  m.79  m.83  m.__  m.__  m.__  m.125  m.132
       _:‖  _:‖  IAC→_:‖  IAC  ___  PAC→_:‖  m.75 →_:‖  →_:‖  IAC→c: HC

                  Introduction
link  a8  a9  a10  e4  e5  e6  e7  e8  j1  j2  cad.ext.  link
       m.132bis  m.133  m.134  m.136  m.143  m.149  m.151  m.155  m.167  m.__  m.183  m.187  m.195(elision)
  →g: HC   HC   IAC→_:‖  →_:‖  →_:‖  HC   IAC→_:HC   IAC →_:HC   HC   HC
```

(continued)

c1   c4   k1   k2   link   f4   g6   f5   g7   f6   g8   cad.ext.   h3   h4   i3   i4

m.___   m.211 m.215 m.___   m.221 m.225 m.229   m.233 m.237 m.241 m.245   m.___   m.___   m.___   m.___ m.___
___   DC; eb: DC; _:_   ___   IAC→_:_   ___   IAC   ___   IAC   ---   ---   ---   ---

Introduction   Codetta
c5   a11   a12   a13   c6   end
m.294 m.___   m.___   m.___
HC   HC   IAC   PAC   PAC

Where in the first fifty measures are there augmented sixth chords? What kind are they?

How do the keys in the exposition after m. 51 differ from what is suggested by the model for sonata form?

Why might Beethoven have chosen to use different bridge material in the recapitulation than the material he used in the exposition?

How does the starting key of the secondary theme in the recapitulation differ from what is suggested by the model for sonata form?

What type of harmonic sequence is heard in mm. 245–249?

Bonus: Give the measure number for an augmented sixth chord in the key of F minor, and identify what type it is.

Name: _____

Homework Assignment 4.6: Listen to the first movement of Fanny Mendelssohn-Hensel's Trio in D minor, Op. 11 and mark its phrase structure directly on the score. Then look at the incomplete phrase diagram below; this diagram may or may not reflect your interpretation. Fill in the blanks with formal labels (e.g. exposition, primary theme, bridge, etc.), cadence types, measure numbers or key areas, as appropriate. Then answer the questions that follow the diagram.

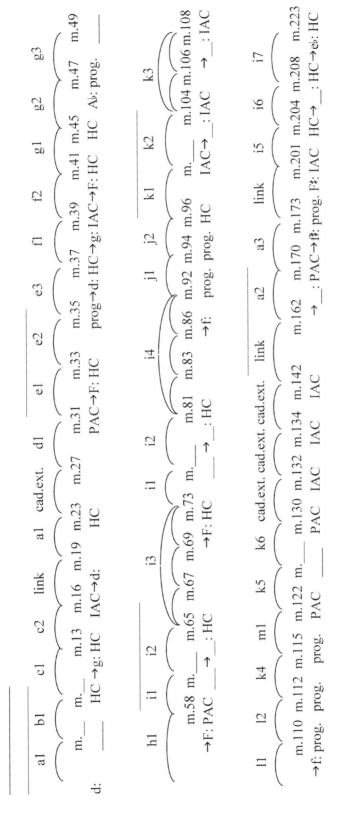

a1 b1 c1 c2 link a1 cad.ext. d1 e1 e2 e3 f1 f2 g1 g2 g3

m.__ m.__ m.13 m.16 m.19 m.23 m.27 m.31 m.33 m.35 m.37 m.39 m.41 m.45 m.47 m.49

d: __ HC →g: HC IAC→d: HC PAC→F: HC prog→d: HC→g: IAC→F: HC HC A♭: prog. ___

h1 i1 i2 i3 i4 j1 j2 k1 k2 k3

m.58 m.__ m.65 m.67 m.69 m.73 m.__ m.81 m.83 m.86 m.92 m.94 m.96 m.__ m.104 m.106 m.108

→F: PAC __→__: HC →F: HC __→__: HC →f: HC →f: prog. prog. HC IAC→__: IAC →__: IAC

l1 l2 k4 m1 k5 k6 cad.ext. cad.ext. cad.ext. link a2 a3 link i5 i6 i7

m.110 m.112 m.115 m.122 m.__ m.130 m.132 m.134 m.142 m.162 m.170 m.173 m.201 m.204 m.208 m.223

→f: prog. prog. PAC ___ PAC IAC IAC IAC →__: PAC→f♯: prog. F♯: IAC HC→__: PAC→f♯: IAC HC→__: HC HC→e♭: HC

(continued)

n1   n2   link   e4   e5   a4   e6   e7   e8   a5   b2   c3   c4   d2   e9   e10

m.227 m.231 link m.235 m.236 m.238 m.243 m.244 m.246 m.253 m.___ m.___ m.264 m.267 m.271 m.275 m.283(elision)

HC prog. →g: IAC→B♭: HC→c: HC prog. →g: HC→a: HC→d: HC ___ HC IAC HC prog. HC →a: HC

link   i8   i9   i10   i8   i11   o1   k7   k8   k9   l3   l4   k10   m2

298   305   307   309   313   317   328   332   340   342   344   346   348   351   358

D: →_:HC   →D: HC   HC   IAC   HC   IAC→_:IAC   →_:IAC   prog.   prog.   prog.   PAC

k11   k12   cad.ext. cad.ext. cad.ext.   a6   a7   cad.ext. cad.ext.

366   368   370   378   382   404   408   end

PAC   IAC   IAC   IAC   concl.   IAC

Where are there chromatic mediant key relationships in this movement?

What is the harmonic analysis of m. 112?

The progressive cadence marked in m. 271 sounds like a deceptive cadence in two important ways. What are they?

The music in mm. 32–35 is divided into two phrases, yet when the same melodic material comes back in mm. 272–275, it's analyzed as one phrase. How could one justify this analysis?

What is the function of the diminished seventh chord in mm. 380–381?

Name: _____

Homework Assignment 5.1: The fourth movement of Brahms' Symphony No. 4 is a variations form, but with a strong overlay of sonata form elements. Listen to it with the score, and then chart the sections and parts in relation to a sonata form model (e.g. Primary Theme, Bridge, Secondary Theme, etc.). Every instance of the ostinato has been accounted for at the bottom of the page. Add formal labels associated with sonata form above the instances of the ostinato, like so:

EXPOSITION

            Primary Theme

  Intro

ostinato: 1–8, 9–16,   17–24, 25–32, 33–40, 41–48, etc. (these are measure numbers)

Note that this movement is not really in sonata form, but rather is just "sonata-like" (it lacks the characteristic tension between key areas in the exposition and its subsequent resolution in the recapitulation). Nevertheless, label the following parts of a sonata form in your graphic representation: introduction (all *three* times!), exposition, primary theme (both times), secondary theme, development, and recapitulation (don't label bridges or closings, and note that the secondary theme only appears in the exposition, not in the recapitulation). Finally, answer the questions at the bottom of the page.

ostinato: mm. 1–8, 9–16, 17–24, 25–32, 33–40, 41–48, 49–56, 57–64, 65–72, 73–80, 81–88, 89–96, 97–104, 105–112, 113–120,

mm. 121–128, 129–136, 137–144, 145–152, 153–160, 161–168, 169–176, 177–184, 185–192, 193–200, 201–208, 209–216, 217–224,

mm. 225–232, 233–240, 241–248 (ostinato breaks after m. 248, coda begins in m. 253)

Is this movement an example of continuous variations or sectional variations? _____

Where in the first 100 measures of this movement is there a descending fifths sequence? Give measure numbers. _____

Name: _____

Homework Assignment 5.2: Listen to the first movement of Mozart's Piano Sonata, K. 331 with the score, and then chart the differences between the theme and each subsequent variation. Use the summary given as Example 5.3 as a model.

Theme – andante grazioso, 6/8, A major, sectional rounded binary form, ♪ ♪♪♪. ♪

Var. I –

Var. II –

Var. III –

Var. IV –

Var. V –

Var. VI –

Name: _____

Homework Assignment 5.3: Go online and download one of the following jazz performances: 1) Miles Davis (trumpet) playing "Just Squeeze Me" (album: *The Legendary Prestige Quintet Sessions*); 2) Bill Evans (piano) playing "Wrap Your Troubles in Dreams" (album: *Interplay*); or 3) John Coltrane (tenor sax) playing "I Hear a Rhapsody" (album: *Lush Life*). Listen to the performance you choose and chart what happens in each chorus of the 32-bar song form (e.g. chorus 1: full ensemble plays head; chorus 2: trumpet solo; chorus 3: solo continues; chorus 4: piano solo; chorus 5: solo continues, etc.).

I listened to _____ by _____ .

Chorus 1: _____

Chorus 2: _____

Chorus 3: _____

Chorus 4: _____

Chorus 5: _____

Chorus 6: _____

Chorus 7: _____

Chorus 8: _____

Chorus 9: _____

(Only one of the three choices above uses nine choruses; if your choice is shorter, strike out the extra blanks.)

Homework Assignment 6.1: Listen to J. S. Bach's Two–Part Invention No. 13 in A Minor while following along with the score, and mark cadence points in the score as you listen. The incomplete phrase diagram given below may or may not reflect your interpretation. Fill in the blanks with cadence types, sequence types, measure numbers or key areas, as appropriate (blanks after arrows are for keys).

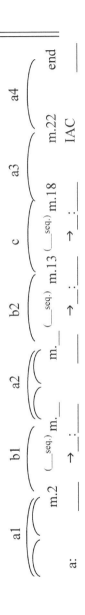

Name: _____

Homework Assignment 6.3: Listen to J. S. Bach's Fugue in B Major from his *The Well-Tempered Clavier*, Book I while following along with the score, and mark cadence points in the score as you listen. The incomplete phrase diagram given below may or may not reflect your interpretation. Fill in the blanks with formal labels (e.g. exposition, episode, etc.), cadence types, sequence types, measure numbers or key areas, as appropriate (blanks before colons are for keys). Be sure to distinguish between real and tonal answers in the appropriate blanks.

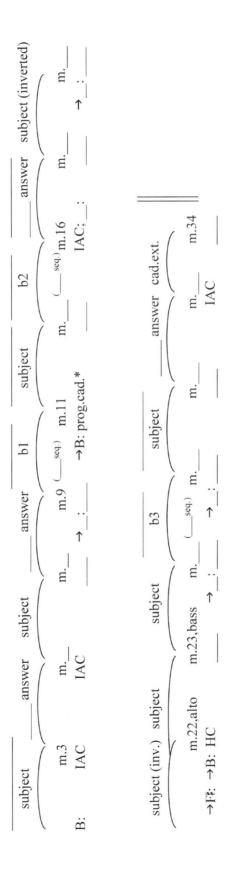

_____ subject _____ _____ answer _____ subject _____ _____ answer _____ b1 _____ subject _____ b2 _____ _____ answer _____ subject (inverted) _____

m.3   answer   subject   m._   m._   m.9 (__seq.) m.11   m._   m.__ (__seq.) m.16   m._   m._

B: IAC   m._   → _: → _: →B: prog.cad.*   IAC; _: → _:

              m.
              IAC

subject (inv.) subject _____ subject _____ b3 _____ subject _____ _____ answer cad.ext. _____

m.22,alto   m.23,bass   m._ (__seq.) m._   m._   m.   m.34

→F♯: →B: HC   → _: → _: IAC

Name: _____

Homework Assignment 6.4: Listen to the fugue from the overture to Handel's *Messiah* while following along with the score, and mark cadence points in the score as you listen. The incomplete phrase diagram of the fugue given below may or may not reflect your interpretation. Fill in the blanks with formal labels (e.g. exposition, episode, etc.), cadence types, sequence types, measure numbers or key areas, as appropriate (blanks before colons are for keys). Be sure to distinguish between real and tonal answers in the appropriate blanks.

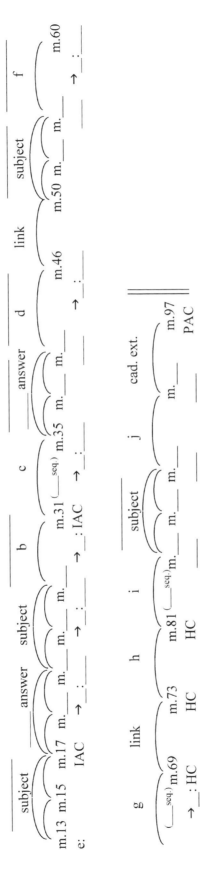

NB: To narrow things down more, the sequences asked for above are in mm. 31–35, 60–64, and 83–85.

Homework Assignment 7.1: Listen to the first movement of "Winter" from Vivaldi's *Four Seasons* and mark its phrase structure directly on the score. Then look at the incomplete phrase diagram below; this diagram may or may not reflect your interpretation. Fill in the blanks with formal labels (i.e. ritornellos and solo sections), cadence types, sequence types, measure numbers or key areas, as appropriate (blanks before colons are for keys).

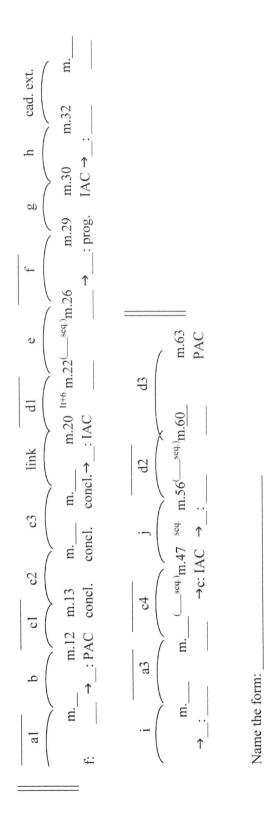

Name the form: _____

Bonus: What type of harmonic sequence is in mm. 51-53? _____

Homework Assignment 7.2: Listen to the first movement of Mozart's Piano Concerto in D major, K. 107 and mark its phrase structure directly on the score. Then look at the incomplete phrase diagram below; this diagram may or may not reflect your interpretation. Fill in the blanks with formal labels (i.e. exposition, primary theme, bridge, etc.), cadence types, sequence types, measure numbers or key areas, as appropriate (blanks before colons are for keys). Note that this diagram does not include the cadenza.

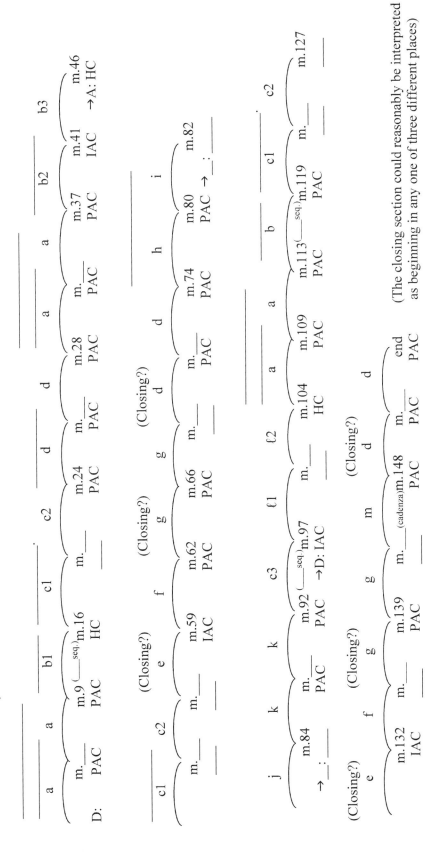

(The closing section could reasonably be interpreted as beginning in any one of three different places)

Homework Assignment 7.3: The first movement of Mozart's Piano Concerto in E♭ major, K. 271 is an expansion of the Classical concerto model in that it has multiple bridge and closing sections. Listen to the movement and mark the formal structure (i.e. the orchestral exposition, primary theme, bridge, etc.) directly on the score. Then look at the incomplete formal diagram below; this diagram may or may not reflect your interpretation. Fill in the blanks with P (primary theme), B1 (1st bridge), B2 (2nd bridge), B3 (3rd bridge), S (secondary theme), C1 (first closing), or C2 (second closing) by comparing the material after m. 62 to the same material in the orchestral exposition. Finally, answer the questions that follow the diagram.

Orchestral Exposition   Solo Exposition   Development

		C1 C2							(solo)	(tutti) (solo)
part:	__	__	__	__	__	__	__	__		
mm.: 1	7	26 34 41	63	69	88	96	135	148	156	162	182 186

Recapitulation

						(cadenza)
__	__	__	__	__	__	
196	202	217	225	251	273	282 292

1. What minor key is found in the development section? _____

2. What type of harmonic sequence is found in mm. 207–208? _____

3. It's also possible to take the beginning of the development section at m. 148 or at m. 156. State your preferred interpretation (i.e. the place where you think the development section begins) and give at least two musical reasons that support your answer.

Name: ____________________

Homework Assignment 7.4: The first movement of Mozart's Clarinet Concerto in A major, K. 622 is an expansion of the Classical concerto model in that it has multiple bridge and closing sections. Listen to the movement and mark the formal structure (i.e. the orchestral exposition, primary theme, bridge, etc.) directly on the score. Then look at the incomplete formal diagram below; this diagram may or may not reflect your interpretation. Fill in the blanks with P (primary theme), B1 (1st bridge), B2 (2nd bridge), S (secondary theme), C1 (first closing), C2 (second closing), and C3 (third closing) by comparing the material after m. 56 to the same material in the orchestral exposition. Then answer the three questions that follow the diagram.

	Orchestral Exposition					Solo Exposition							Development				
part:	P	B1	C1	C2	C3	___	___	___	___	___	___	___	(solo)	(tutti)	(solo)	(tutti)	(solo)
mm.:	1	16	25	39	49	57	78	100	128	134	154	164	172	192	194	227	248

Recapitulation						
___	___	___	___	___	___	(cadenza)/___
251	272	292	316	322	343	352

1. What key is tonicized in mm. 82–90? ___________

2. What keys are found in mm. 172–250 (the development section)? List them in order: __, __, __, __, __, __, and __.

3. The music in mm. 86–94 sounds very thematic. What problems are there with calling it the second theme? List two problems:

Name: _____

Homework Assignment 7.5: Listen to the first movement of Mozart's Flute Concerto in G major, K. 313 and mark its phrase structure directly on the score. Then look at the incomplete phrase diagram below; this diagram may or may not reflect your interpretation. Fill in the blanks with formal labels (i.e. exposition, primary theme, bridge, etc.), cadence types, sequence types, measure numbers or key areas, as appropriate (blanks before colons are for keys). Finally, answer the questions that follow the diagram. Note that this diagram does not include the cadenza.

_____

a1	a2	cad.ext.	cad.ext.	b	c1	c2	d1	d2	e1	f1	f2	g1	g1	cad.ext.	a1
G:	m._	m.7	m.8	m.10	m.12	m.14	m.16	m.17	m.19	m.23	m._	m._	m.27	m.28	m.29	m.30	m._
	___	HC	HC	IAC	___	HC	DC	___	prog.	prog.	PAC	___	___	___	PAC	PAC	PAC	___

_____

a2	cad.ext.	cad.ext.	h	cad.ext.	g1	link	i1	j1	i2	j2	j2	j3	k1	c1	c2
m.37	m.38	m.40	m.42	m.44	m.45	m.46	m.48	m.49	m.52	m.53	m.54	m.55	m.57	m.59	m.60
HC	HC	IAC	IAC	PAC	PAC→	_:PAC	IAC	IAC→	IAC→	_:IAC	IAC	IAC	prog.	HC	HC	HC

ℓ1	ℓ2	ℓ3	m1	c3	c4	d3	d4	e2	f3	f3	f4	cad.ext.	a3	n1	g2	g2
m.62	m.64	m.66	m.69	m.70	m.72	m.73	m.75	m.79	m._	m.83	m.88	m.91	m.94	m.100	m.101	m.102
IAC	HC→b:	HC→D:	PAC	PAC	DC	prog.	prog.	PAC	___	___	___	PAC	IAC	PAC	PAC	PAC

_____

cad.ext.	o1	p1	q1	r1	g3	g3	cad.ext.	o2	p2	q2	r2	s	p3	t1	t2	t3
m.103	m.105	m.107	m.109	m.111	m.112	m.113	m.114	m.116	m.118	m.120	m.122	m.125	m.127	m.129	m.131	m.133
PAC	IAC	d: IAC→	_:IAC	IAC	PAC	PAC	IAC	IAC	IAC→	_:IAC	IAC	___	___ ; a: IAC; D: PAC; G: PAC;

(continued)

t4 u1 u2 v o3 o3 o4 a1 a2 cad.ext. cad.ext. h cad.ext. g1 link. i3 j4

m.135 m.136 m.138 m.142 m.144 m.146 m.149 m.___ m.155 m.156 m.158 m.160 m.162 m.163 m.164 m.166 m.167
C: PAC; a: IAC; G: IAC HC HC HC PAC ___ HC IAC IAC PAC PAC→ :IAC→___ :IAC IAC

i4 j5 j5 p1 c3 c4 ℓ4 ℓ5 ℓ6 m2 c3 c4 d3 d4 e2 f1 f1

m.170 m.171 m.172 m.175 m.177 m.178 m.180 m.182 m.184 m.187 m.188 m.189 m.191 m.193 m.197 m.___ m.201
→G: IAC IAC IAC HC HC HC IAC HC HC →e: HC→G: PAC PAC DC prog. prog. PAC ___

f5 cad.ext. a3 n2 g1 g1 cad.ext.

m.206 m.209 m.212 (cadenza) m.216 m.217 m.218 end
___ PAC IAC PAC PAC PAC PAC PAC

1. What is the form of this movement? _____

2. What type of harmonic sequence is in mm. 127–135? _____

3. Because there is a second theme presented in the orchestral exposition, and because mm. 60–70 present new material that was not included in that exposition, one has to decide whether or not that material belongs to the second theme or to some other part of the form. Why does it make sense to consider it part of the second theme in this movement?

Name: _____

Homework Assignment 7.6: Listen to the first movement of Mendelssohn's Violin Concerto, Op. 64 and mark its phrase structure directly on the score. Then look at the incomplete phrase diagram below; this diagram may or may not reflect your interpretation. Fill in the blanks with formal labels (i.e. exposition, primary theme, bridge, etc.), cadence types, sequence types, measure numbers or key areas, as appropriate (blanks before colons are for keys). Finally, answer the questions that follow the diagram. Note that this diagram does not include the cadenza.

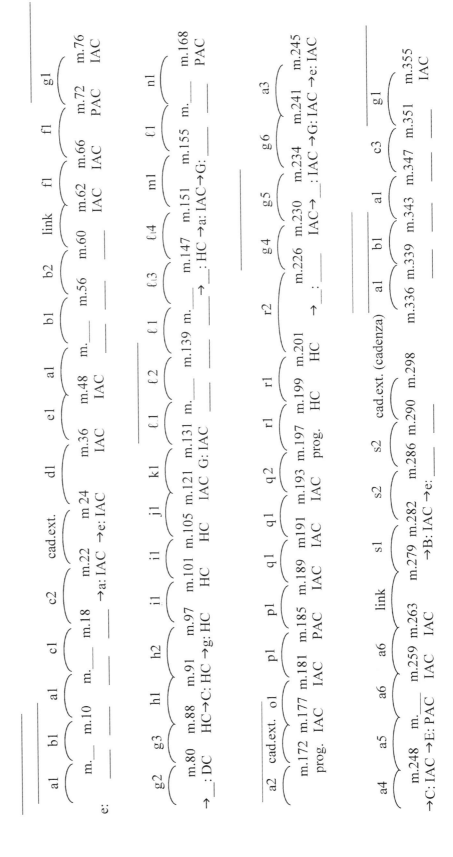

____
a1 b1 a1 c1 c2 cad.ext. d1 e1 a1 b1 b2 link f1 f1 g1
m.__ m.10 m.__ m.18 m.22 m 24 m.36 m.48 m.__ m.56 m.60 m.62 m.66 m.72 m.76
e: ____ ____ →a: IAC →e: IAC IAC IAC ____ ____ IAC IAC PAC IAC

g2 g3 h1 h2 i1 i1 j1 k1 ℓ1 ℓ2 ℓ1 ℓ3 ℓ4 m1 ℓ1 n1
m.80 m.88 m.91 m.97 m.101 m.105 m.121 m.131 m.__ m.139 m.147 m.151 m.155 m.__ m.168
→_: DC HC→C: HC →g: HC HC HC IAC G: IAC →_: HC →a: IAC→G: _ : HC →a: IAC→G: PAC

a2 cad.ext. o1 p1 p1 q1 q1 q2 r1 r1 r2 g4 g5 g6 a3
m.172 m.177 m.181 m.185 m.189 m191 m.193 m.197 m.199 m.201 m.226 m.230 m.234 m.241 m.245
prog. IAC IAC PAC IAC IAC IAC IAC prog. HC HC →_:_ IAC→_:_ IAC→G: IAC →e: IAC

a4 a5 a6 a6 a6 link s1 s2 s2 s2 cad.ext. (cadenza) a1 b1 a1 c3 g1
m.248 m.__ m.259 m.263 m.279 m.282 m.286 m.290 m.298 m.336 m.339 m.343 m.347 m.351 m.355
→C: IAC →E: PAC IAC IAC →B: IAC →e: ____ IAC

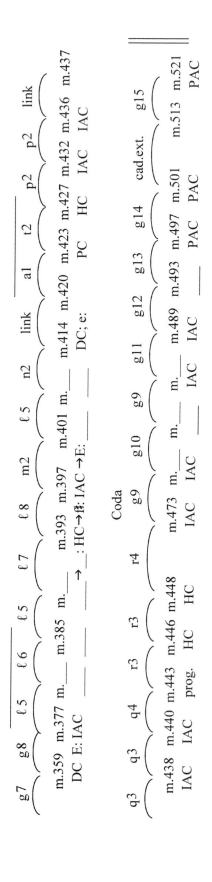

g7   g8   ℓ5   ℓ6   ℓ5   ℓ7   ℓ8   m2   ℓ5   n2   link   a1   t2   p2   p2   link

m.359   m.377 m.___   m.385   m.___   m.393   m.397   m.401 m.___   m.414   m.420   m.423   m.427   m.432   m.436   m.437

DC E: IAC   → ___ : HC→f♯: IAC →E: ___   DC; e: PC   HC   IAC   IAC

Coda

q3   q3   q4   r3   r3   r4   g9   g10   g9   g11   g12   g13   g14   cad.ext.   g15

m.438   m.440   m.443   m.446 m.448   m.473   m.___   m.___   m.489   m.493   m.497   m.501   m.513   m.521

IAC   IAC   prog.   HC   HC   IAC   IAC   IAC   IAC   PAC   PAC   PAC   PAC   PAC

1. How should one label the five-note chord on the downbeat of m. 88? Give both a chord name and a Roman numeral: _____,

    _____

2. What are the five harmonies in mm.113–121? Give both chord names and Roman numerals: _____, _____, _____,

    _____, _____ m.113, m.115, m.117, m.119, m.221

3. In what ways does the material in mm. 377–385 fit the definition of a sentence? In what ways does it fit the definition of a period?

4. This movement is not in Classical concerto form. What are two important ways in which the formal structure of this movement is different than that of a movement in Classical concerto form?

Homework Assignment 7.7: Listen to the first movement of Haydn's Trumpet Concerto in E♭ Major and mark its phrase structure directly on the score. Then look at the incomplete phrase diagram below; this diagram may or may not reflect your interpretation. Fill in the blanks with formal labels (i.e. exposition, primary theme, bridge, etc.), cadence types, sequence types, measure numbers or key areas, as appropriate (blanks before colons are for keys). Finally, answer the questions on the back of the page. Note that this diagram does not include the cadenza.

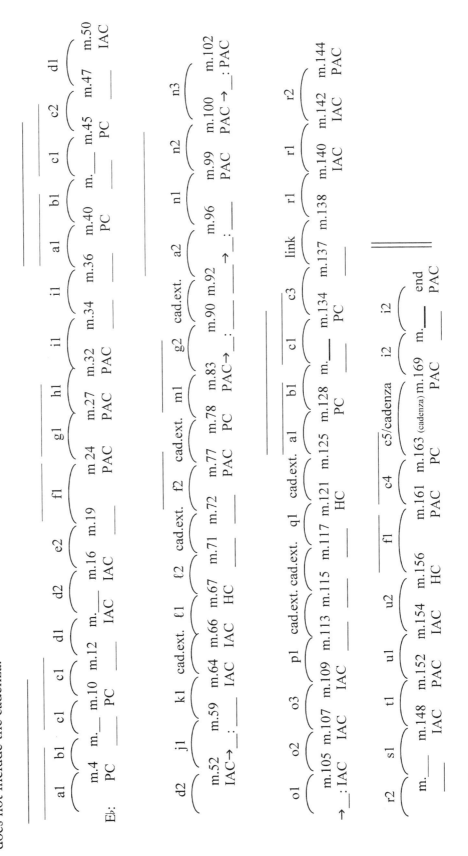

(continued)

1. What is the form of this movement? _____

2. Measures 69–70 are a common substitution for a descending fifth sequence; it only differs from a descending fifth sequence by two notes in the viola. What is the harmonic analysis of these measures? Name the four chords in m. 69 and the first two chords in m. 70 (the sequence breaks after that), then identify which two notes in the viola part could be changed to make this a descending fifth sequence, and how they would be changed.

3. What is the harmonic progression in mm. 110–115? Give both chord names and Roman numerals.

chord name: _____ _____ _____ _____ _____ _____

Roman numeral: _____ _____ _____ _____ _____ _____

measure: 110   111   112   113   114   115

Name: _____

Homework Assignment 8.1: Listen to the fourth movement of Mozart's Symphony No. 35, and mark its phrase structure directly on the score. Then look at the incomplete phrase diagram below; this diagram may or may not reflect your interpretation. Fill in the blanks with formal labels (i.e. exposition, primary theme, etc.), cadence types, sequence types, measure numbers or key areas, as appropriate.

Exposition/Primary Th.

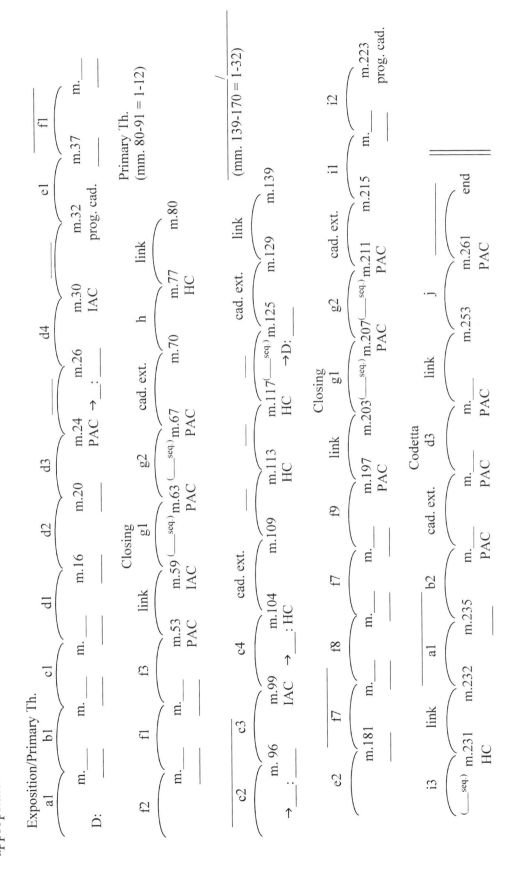

a1 b1 c1 d1 d2 d3 d4 e1 f1

D: m.__ m.__ m.__ m.16 m.20 m.24 m.26 m.30 m.32 m.37 m.__
PAC → _: IAC   prog. cad.

f2 f1 f3 link g1 g2 cad. ext. h link

Closing

m.__ m.__ m.53 m.59 $\xrightarrow{seq.}$ m.63 $\xrightarrow{seq.}$ m.67 m.70 m.77 m.80
PAC   IAC   PAC   PAC   HC

c2 c3 c4 cad. ext. cad. ext. link

→ _: m.96 m.99 m.104 m.109 m.113 m.117 $\xrightarrow{seq.}$ m.125 m.129 m.139
IAC → _:HC   HC   →D: __

Primary Th. (mm. 80-91 = 1-12)
(mm. 139-170 = 1-32)

e2 f7 f8 f9 link g1 g2 cad. ext. i1 i2

Closing

m.181 m.__ m.__ m.__ m.197 m.203 $\xrightarrow{seq.}$ m.207 $\xrightarrow{seq.}$ m.211 m.215 m.__ m.223
PAC   PAC   PAC   PAC   prog. cad.

i3 link a1 b2 cad. ext. d3 link j

Codetta

$\xrightarrow{seq.}$ m.231 m.232 m.235 m.__ m.__ m.__ m.253 m.261 end
HC   PAC   PAC   PAC   PAC

Name: _____

Homework Assignment 8.2: Listen to the third movement of Mozart's Piano Sonata, K. 333 and mark its phrase structure directly on the score. Then look at the incomplete phrase diagram below; this diagram may or may not reflect your interpretation. Fill in the blanks with formal labels (i.e. exposition, primary theme, etc.), cadence types, sequence types, measure numbers or key areas, as appropriate. Then answer the five questions that follow the diagram.

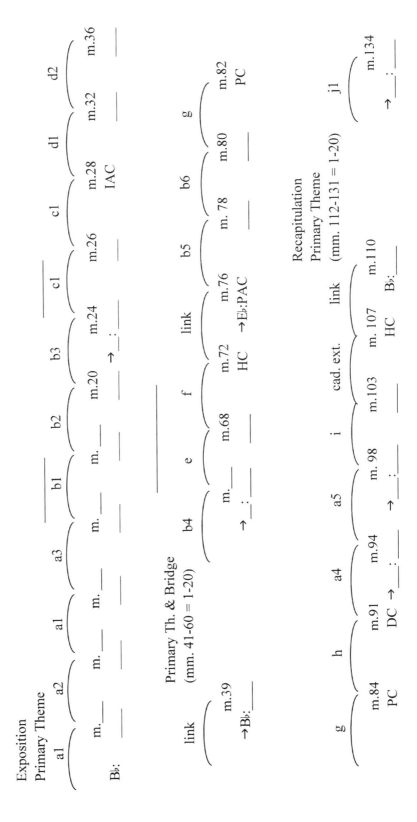

Exposition
Primary Theme

a1 a2 a1 a3   b1   b2   b3 c1   c1 d1 d2

m.___ m.___ m.___   m.___ m.___ m.20 m.24   m.26 m.28 m.32 m.36
B♭: ___ ___ ___   ___ ___   → ___: ___ IAC ___ ___

Primary Th. & Bridge
(mm. 41-60 = 1-20)

link   b4   e   f   link   b5   b6   g

m.39   m.___ m.68 m.72 m.76   m. 78 m.80 m.82
→B♭: ___   → ___: ___ HC →E♭:PAC   ___ ___ PC

g   h   a4   a5   i   cad. ext.   link   Recapitulation
                                                 Primary Theme
                                                 (mm. 112-131 = 1-20)   j1

m.84 m.91 m.94 m. 98 m.103   m.107   m.110   m.134
PC DC → ___: ___ → ___: ___   HC   B♭:___   → ___:

(continued)

1. What is the form of this movement? _____

2. There is a descending fifth sequence in the cadenza; give the exact measure numbers in which it begins and ends. _____ _____

3. What is the Roman numeral analysis of the two harmonies in m. 63 (assuming that A is a passing tone)? _____ _____

4. What is the Roman numeral analysis of the harmony in m. 198? _____

5. What is the Roman numeral analysis of the harmony in m. 215? _____

Name: _____

Homework Assignment 8.3: Listen to the fourth movement of Haydn's Symphony No. 101 and mark its phrase structure directly on the score. Then look at the incomplete phrase diagram below; this diagram may or may not reflect your interpretation. Fill in the blanks with formal labels (i.e. exposition, primary theme, etc.), cadence types, sequence types, measure numbers or key areas, as appropriate (blanks before colons are for keys). Then answer the question that follows the diagram.

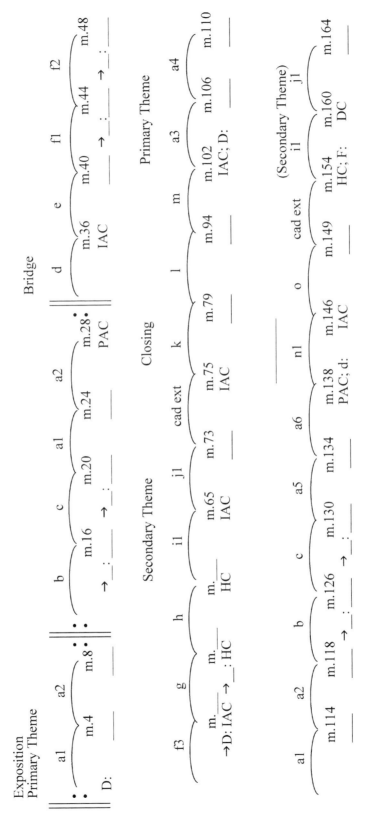

(continued)

Fugato and Recap-like Coda

p1	p2	n2	n3	cad ext	a7	a8	a9	cad ext	a10	link
m.168	m.172	m.176	m.180	m.188	m.193	m.198	m.203	m.205	m.209	m._
g: IAC	F: PAC	g: PAC	d: HC		D: HC	IAC →	→_: HC	IAC	→e: IAC	→G: IAC

a11	cad ext	q	cad ext	a12	a13	a1	a2	cad ext	r	s
m.218	m.220	m.229	m.233	m._	m._	m.253	m.257	m.261	m.270	m.274
→e: HC	PAC	→D: HC	IAC	HC	PAC	___	___	PAC	PAC	IAC

cad ext
end
PAC

What type of sequence is in mm. 218-225? _____

Homework Assignment 8.4: Listen to the second movement of Beethoven's Piano Sonata, Op. 13 and mark its phrase structure directly on the score. Then look at the incomplete phrase diagram below; this diagram may or may not reflect your interpretation. Fill in the blanks with formal labels (A, B, C, etc.), cadence types, measure numbers or key areas, as appropriate. Then answer the questions that follow the diagram.

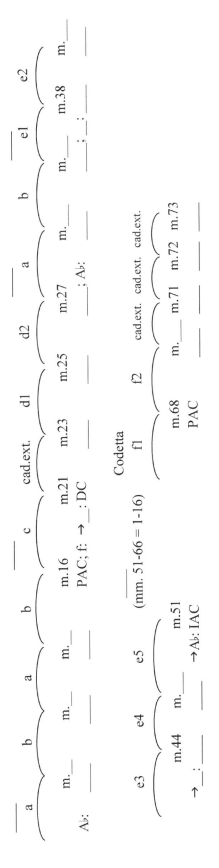

1. What is the form of this movement? _____

2. What harmonic sequence underpins phrase b? _____

3. The diagram above suggests that the phrase structure of mm. 51–66 and mm. 1–16 is the same, and that is true, but how are those measures different? In particular, what about the phrase ending in mm. 65–66 seems to demand that a codetta follow?

Name: _____

Homework Assignment 8.5: Listen to the second movement of Mozart's *Eine kleine Nachtmusik* and mark its phrase structure directly on the score. Then look at the incomplete phrase diagram below; this diagram may or may not reflect your interpretation. Fill in the blanks with formal labels (A, B, C, etc.), cadence types, measure numbers or key areas, as appropriate. Then answer the questions that follow the diagram.

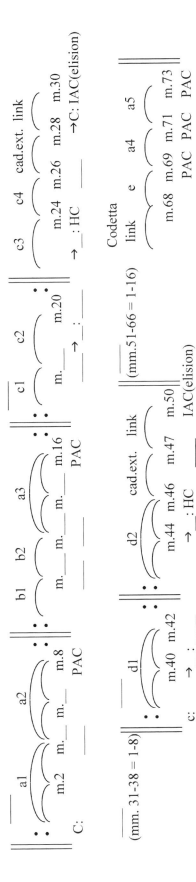

1. What is the form of this movement? _____

2. What is the form of the A section? _____

3. What harmonic sequence underpins the first half of phrase c3? _____

4. What harmonic sequence underpins the first half of phrase d2? _____

5. What kind of non-chord tones in the first violin part embellish the final two tonic chords (mm. 71 and 73)? _____

Homework Assignment 8.6: Listen to the fourth movement of Mozart's *Eine kleine Nachtmusik* and mark its phrase structure directly on the score. Then look at the incomplete phrase diagram below; this diagram may or may not reflect your interpretation. Fill in the blanks with cadence types, measure numbers or key areas, as appropriate. Then answer the questions that follow the diagram.

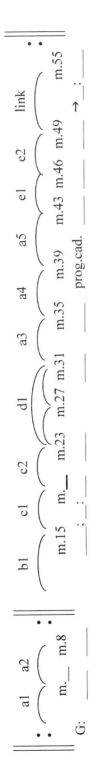

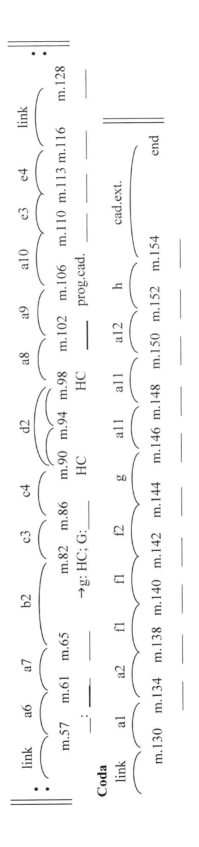

1. This movement can be viewed as a sonata–rondo (the label "Rondo" provided by Mozart really refers to the style of the movement, not its actual form). Write in formal labels above the phrases that reflect this interpretation (be sure to place the labels precisely).

2. What two things about the exposition here differ from what is suggested by the model?

3. What two things about the recapitulation here differ from what is suggested by the model?